IMAGES
of Sport

WIGAN
RUGBY LEAGUE
FOOTBALL CLUB

Determination and concentration – the hallmark of Shaun Edwards. In 1988, he became the youngest player to captain a Challenge Cup-winning side at Wembley.

IMAGES
of Sport

WIGAN
RUGBY LEAGUE
FOOTBALL CLUB

Compiled by
Graham Morris

TEMPUS

First published 2001
Copyright © Graham Morris, 2001

Tempus Publishing Limited
The Mill, Brimscombe Port,
Stroud, Gloucestershire, GL5 2QG

ISBN 0 7524 2299 5

Typesetting and origination by
Tempus Publishing Limited
Printed in Great Britain by
Midway Colour Print, Wiltshire

Front cover illustration: Wigan captain Joe Egan is carried shoulder-high by his jubilant team, as they celebrate their 1948 Rugby League Challenge Cup final victory over Bradford Northern at Wembley Stadium.

Boulevard Voices	Raymond Fletcher	0 7524 2190 5
Bradford Bulls RLFC	Robert Gate	0 7524 1896 3
Castleford RLFC	David Smart	0 7524 1895 5
Featherstone Rovers RLFC	Ron Bailey	0 7524 2295 2
Halifax RLFC	Andrew Hardcastle	0 7524 1831 9
Headingley Voices	Phil Caplan	0 7524 1822 X
Hunslet RLFC	Les Hoole	0 7524 1641 3
Leeds RLFC	Phil Caplan & Les Hoole	0 7524 1140 3
Leeds RLFC: 100 Greats	Phil Caplan & Peter Smith	0 7524 2225 1
Salford RLFC	Graham Morris	0 7524 1897 1
Salford RLFC: 100 Greats	Graham Morris	0 7524 2196 4
Sheffield Eagles RLFC	John Cornwell	0 7524 1830 0
St Helens RLFC	Alex Service	0 7524 1883 1
Warrington RLFC	Gary Slater & Eddie Fuller	0 7524 1870 X
Yorkshire RL	Les Hoole	0 7524 1881 5

Contents

Ernie Ashcroft (left) and Eric Ashton were both outstanding centres whose careers overlapped in the late 1950s, Ashton effectively replacing his illustrious predecessor. Both of them captained Wigan.

Acknowledgements

Whenever a compilation such as this is published, there is, inevitably, a list of people to express gratitude to. Individuals who have provided help, both recently and in the past, are: Timothy Auty, Mrs Brian Baker, Billy Blan, Trevor Delaney, Mike Flynn, Bill Francis, Robert Gate, Graham Gerrard, Geoff Hurst, Michael Latham, John Riding, Mike Rylance and Irvin Saxton. My sincere thanks to the following organizations and their representatives: *Daily Telegraph*; Lancashire Publications Ltd (*Rugby Leaguer, Wigan Evening Post, Wigan Observer*) particularly Carol Turner and Gary Brunskill, who allowed use of several photographs including those of Frank Orrell; League Publications Ltd (*Rugby League Express, Rugby League World*); Wigan Heritage Service; Wigan Local History Library; and, of course, the Wigan Warriors Rugby League Club for their help and support, particularly Lee Addison, Gordon Harrison and Mary Sharkey. Thanks, also, to Sportsphotos Ltd of Scarborough, who provided the excellent photograph (by Richard Sellers) of Shaun Edwards that appears on page two, and to Topps UK Ltd for their kind permission to reproduce the Merlin trading cards and Merlin stickers that appear in chapter six. The origination of some photographs, particularly the older ones, is unknown. Wherever possible I have attempted to contact copyright holders for their permission to reproduce them.

Introduction

Attempting to do justice to the wonderful galaxy of stars that have brought pride to the cherry and white of Wigan for the past 130 years has been both challenging and enjoyable. It was challenging because I often had the feeling that I was trying to pour the proverbial quart into a pint pot. Quite simply, the exploits of such an impressive 'Hall of Fame' of players – a list that would stand comparison with any club, irrespective of sport or country – could well have filled two volumes of the Tempus *Images of Sport* series! The question I continually asked myself was 'what do I leave out?' For similar reasons, however, it was an enjoyable experience. To trawl through such a catalogue of success and cherry-pick (forgive the obvious pun!) the best of the best was, in truth, an embarrassment of riches. Along the way, Wigan has appeared in a record-making 26 Challenge Cup finals, including an incredible 22 at Wembley. In total, 100 major trophy triumphs have kept the Wigan display cabinet well stocked over the years. How many other clubs, I wonder, could make a similar boast?

The story of Wigan Rugby League Football Club does not begin, however, in the land of 'milk and honey'. At the time that their representative – club secretary Ellis Wardle – voted in favour of joining the breakaway Northern Union (forerunner of the Rugby League) at the historic meeting in the George Hotel, Huddersfield, on 29 August 1895, they had achieved very little on the field. Playing on a pitch in Prescott Street – their fourth home – they had enjoyed only moderate success in the preceding years, consistently finishing mid-table in the Lancashire Club Championship. It was to be the club's relocation, seven years later in 1902 to grazing land known locally as 'Joe Hill's Field', that heralded the beginning of Wigan's dominance in the sport. Their new enclosure, named Central Park, was a venue that was to become famous throughout the sporting world. That move accomplished, the committee then began a massive recruitment drive, scouring the country, and beyond, in a bid to create a team that would attract the spectators onto its vast terraces. The names of those early Central Park idols are now part of the rich tapestry of the club. Indeed, four of them were enshrined for many years through the inscribed stone blocks situated under the former Central Park pavilion: Jimmy Leytham, Bert Jenkins, Charlie Seeling and Johnny Thomas. Their arrival brought unprecedented success for the Wigan public to feast upon during the years before the First World War, setting a standard for perfection that has been strived for by Wigan officialdom ever since.

Whilst Wigan has never been far from the forefront over the years, finishing outside the Championship top ten on just nine occasions since the First World War, it could be argued there have been four outstanding combinations in the club's history. The aforementioned line-up led by Leytham was the first, the others having paraded their wares in three glorious epochs since the end of the Second World War. In the immediate post-war years, the Joe Egan/Ken Gee-inspired side set new standards and, for seven glorious seasons, were seemingly unstoppable. As that outfit aged, the board of directors performed the difficult feat of moving almost seamlessly into the next generation of players, as Billy Boston and company made Wembley their second home. The fourth great period arrived, after the comparatively barren years of the 1970s, when a new four-man board – Jack Hilton, Tom Rathbone, Jack Robinson, and Maurice Lindsay – took control of club affairs in 1982. The old cliché that 'the rest is history' was never more accurate. They showed a desire and fervour to succeed that would have made the 1902 committee proud! Eight successive wins at Wembley, to say nothing of a clean sweep of just about everything else on offer, showed that the modern board cared very passionately indeed about the legacy that had passed into their hands.

Conspicuous by its absence from the above list, is the time when the truly amazing Jim Sullivan was the 'King' of Wigan – and just about everywhere else – during the inter-war years of the 1920s and '30s. Almost paradoxically, despite the great man's presence, success was limited compared to those other wonderful teams, although three Championships and two Challenge Cup wins may argue otherwise. At many clubs, that would be hailed as a 'Golden Era' – a measure of the high standard set at Wigan.

It is not the intention of this publication to furnish the reader with a comprehensive history of the Wigan Rugby League Club. You will, nonetheless, find yourself conveyed on a voyage that traces the highs and lows of one of the most famous sporting organizations in Britain. As well as bringing to life the years when exciting players like Leytham, Sullivan, Johnny Ring, Gee, Egan, Boston, Eric Ashton, Ellery Hanley and Shaun Edwards, ruled the roost, we pay due homage to the early performers who helped create the aura that surrounds the Wigan club today. How many people, for example, know the name of Ned Bullough, the only player to appear for England at Rugby Union whilst with Wigan? Recognition is also accorded to the modern heroes; the Wigan Warriors, who now entertain the crowds in the magnificent new JJB Stadium in the gladiatorial atmosphere that is Super League.

I have divided the book into six chronological chapters, each covering a specific period in the history of this magnificent club. You could say that the final chapter, called 'The Maurice Lindsay Years', is incomplete, as the subject of that title continues to oversee the affairs of Wigan in his capacity as club chairman. Managing a club such as Wigan is never a one-person operation, but the influence of Lindsay during the past two decades has been immense, the team reaching such heights that it is difficult to imagine anybody could emulate them. The icing on the cake of achievement was to bring the World Club Championship to Britain on three occasions, the pinnacle of which was that memorable victory over Brisbane Broncos at the ANZ stadium in 1994.

Although the 'midnight oil' has been required on more than one occasion along the way, this book has been a joy to compile. I sincerely hope that you find it as rewarding to read.

Graham Morris
Worsley, September 2001.

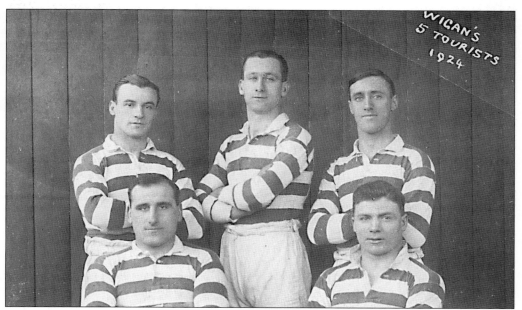

Wigan's five tourists to Australia and New Zealand in 1924. From left to right, back row: Danny Hurcombe, Johnny Ring, Tommy Howley. Front row: Jack Price, Jim Sullivan. Ring scored 23 tries in only 15 matches, whilst Sullivan's 84 goals was a tour record at the time.

One

Folly Field
to Central Park
1872-1920

The original Wigan Rugby Club, formed in November 1872 by members of Wigan Cricket
Club, played at Folly Field, adjoining Upper Dicconson Street. They amalgamated with
Upholland in October 1876, becoming Wigan & District Football Club, but financial strife
brought their demise in February 1878. The roots of today's Wigan Warriors side began in
September 1879 with the creation of Wigan Wasps at The Dicconson Arms, by members of the
local Hare & Hounds Harriers, a field being used at Upper Dicconson Street. The 'Wasps' tag
was dropped in 1881, the club moving in 1886 to a ground at Prescott Street, vacated by Wigan
Cricket Club. This 1885 team displays the Wigan Union Charity Cup, having defeated Haigh
in the final during April, by two tries to one. This trophy was the first to be won by Wigan
when, two years earlier, they beat Pagefield in the inaugural final.

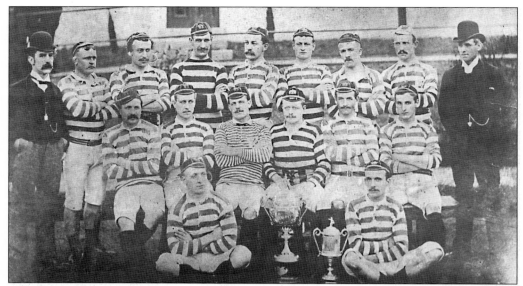

The Wigan team in 1889/90. From left to right, back row: J. Underwood (umpire), J. Lowe, Tom Brayshaw, J. Hatten, Jim Slevin, Jimmy Halliwell, Billy Atkinson, Ned Bullough, J. Bibby (reserve). Middle row: J. Telford, Ellis Wardle, Dick Seddon, Jack Anderton, E. Dempsey, Robert Seddon. Front row: Billy Halliwell, J. Mitchinson. The trophies are for winning the West Lancashire Championship (left) when, unbeaten, they headed the table by 12 points from runners-up Walkden, and the Wigan Union Charity Cup. The latter was secured after defeating major rivals of that period, Aspull, by three tries to two in a final played in pouring rain during May 1890.

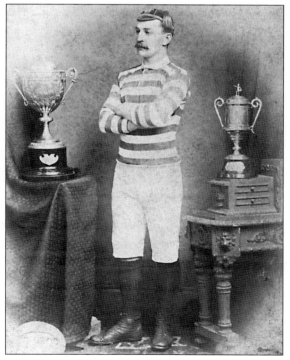

Three-quarter Jim Slevin, seen with the West Lancashire Championship (left) and Wigan Union Charity Cup, was one of Wigan's most outstanding players of the early years. He played in the first match under the Wigan Wasps moniker at home to St Lawrence's (Chorley) on 8 November 1879 and, as team captain, the opening fixture at Prescott Street in September 1886 against Wakefield Trinity. He also led Wigan in their historic meeting with the Maori touring side on 17 December 1888. As the first international rugby team to tour Great Britain, they attracted 8,000 curious spectators to Prescott Street. Having retired in the 1891 close season, he returned to assist the club against St Helens in October 1897 for his only Northern Union game. Appointed as skipper once more, he was on the wrong end of a 17-7 score line.

Wigan forwards Billy Atkinson and Ned Bullough with the Lancashire side that took the county title in 1890/91, before a match against the Rest of England at Whalley Range in April 1891. From left to right, back row: Tom Craven (Salford), Tom Rothwell (Swinton), John Berry (Tyldesley), Bill McCutcheon (Oldham), Jim Pyke (St Helens Recs), Tom Kent (Salford), J. Strang (Liverpool). Middle row: E.H. Flower (Broughton), T. Whittaker (Manchester), Jim Valentine (Swinton), Atkinson, Tom Melladew (Rochdale Hornets), Tom Coop (Leigh). Front row: Bullough, Dai Gwynn (Oldham), Billy Cross (St Helens), R.P. Wilson (Liverpool Old Boys). Bullough is the only Wigan player to represent England at Rugby Union (three caps in 1892) and he and Atkinson are the only two from the club to appear in the annual North of England versus South clashes.

Bill Yates was a signing from local rivals Aspull – who had just disbanded – in 1895, making his debut in the club's first Northern Union fixture at Broughton Rangers on 7 September 1895, claiming Wigan's first try under the new code in a 9-0 win. It was during that inaugural Northern Union season that he earned his two appearances for Lancashire (in whose jersey he is pictured). A sound, work-manlike forward, he went on to appear in 162 matches for the club.

The ambitious move to Central Park, which hosted its first Wigan match on 6 September 1902 against Batley, also signalled a change in the fortunes of the team. The previous season, the club had won the Lancashire League – their first honour under the Northern Union banner – and the committee was intent on building on that success. The Pavilion – seen here – opened in September 1909, the famous inscription often misleading visitors into thinking that 1909 was the year the ground itself had started life. This picture was taken in August 1958, before a match with Hunslet.

W. ANDERSON, Wigan.

From Rugby to Ross or Ballriggan
You won't find a small'un or big'un
More cute in his tricks,
More neat in his kicks
Than the spry little member for
Wigan.

Billy Anderson – lovingly caricatured here – was one of the club's first acquisitions after the move to Central Park. A diminutive half-back, he made his debut against Leigh on 27 September 1902, Wigan's third match at their new ground. He appeared in their first final under Northern Union rules as a member of the team that defeated Leigh 8-0 in the replayed 1905 Lancashire Cup final. A 'Will o' the Wisp' character, Anderson was signed from the Morecambe club and played 149 times for Wigan. He made one appearance for Lancashire, against Cheshire at Runcorn in October 1904.

These two illustrations are from the series of 472 cigarette cards of 'Noted Footballers' by Cope Brothers of Liverpool, issued in 1909. Classy Welsh half Johnny Thomas arrived from Cardiff Rugby Union Club in December 1904, and appeared in 388 matches for Wigan, contributing 108 tries and 439 goals. He formed the half-back combination with Billy Anderson for the first Lancashire Cup success of 1905, enjoying three further wins in that competition, and was in the side that captured Wigan's initial Championship in 1908/09. At representative level, he played for Great Britain on 10 occasions, five of them during the Northern Union's first tour to Australia and New Zealand in 1910. He also represented Wales 8 times and was adopted by Lancashire, appearing in 7 county matches.

When Wigan appeared in their first Championship final in 1909, Dick Ramsdale scored his side's only try, a crucial effort in a narrow 7-3 win over Oldham at Salford. He also earned winners' medals in the Lancashire Cup final victories of 1908, 1909 and 1912. A powerfully-built forward, signed from local rugby, he made his Wigan debut in September 1905, and appeared in 313 matches for the Cherry and Whites. A tourist in 1910 and 1914, he represented Great Britain on 9 occasions, England on 5, and Lancashire 10. In 1921, he was the recipient of a testimonial, shared with Johnny Thomas and Bert Jenkins.

13

The Leytham/Jenkins/Todd/Miller quartet formed a three-quarters line famed in the game's history. Jimmy Leytham transferred from his native Lancaster club in December 1903 for £80, captaining Wigan to some of the greatest triumphs of that era, including the first Championship in 1908/09. Known as 'Gentleman Jim' due to his sporting manner, he was an outstanding winger, leading the Northern Union try charts three times. In 1909/10, his 47 touchdowns equalled the Wigan club record set by Joe Miller the previous season. His six in a match against Merthyr Tydfil in February 1910 was another milestone at the club. He scored an impressive 11 tries in 7 appearances for Great Britain and was in the first touring side in 1910. Leytham represented England (5 times) and Lancashire (11). He played 280 matches for Wigan, scoring 258 tries and 267 goals.

Welshman Bert Jenkins joined Wigan from the Mountain Ash Rugby Union Club, twelve months after Jimmy Leytham, and the two built a formidable partnership on Wigan's flank. On Boxing Day 1907, Jenkins created a short-lived club record as the first Wigan player to notch five tries, against Bradford Northern at Central Park. He was in the first two touring parties to the Antipodes in 1910 and 1914, making 14 appearances for Great Britain from 1907 to 1914. He gained consolation for missing a potential Welsh Rugby Union cap by representing his country 11 times under the Northern Union code, and was claimed by Lancashire for 12 county matches. In addition to providing numerous try-scoring opportunities for Leytham, he bagged a personal tally of 182 for Wigan from 389 outings.

B. JENKINS.
Wigan F. C. & British N. U. Team.

Lance Todd was recognised in his own country as a five-eighth (stand-off half) when he arrived in Britain with the pioneering New Zealand tourists in 1907. Wigan signed him during the tour, and he became an outstanding centre, appearing in 185 matches for the club. Sharing in Wigan's inaugural Championship success in 1908/09, he was also a member of the first Wigan Challenge Cup final line-up, which lost to Broughton Rangers in 1911. During November 1910, he played twice for Lancashire, when his aggregate two tries and two goals helped seal the county title. In 1914, he transferred, unexpectedly, to Dewsbury, later achieving legendary status as team manager of Salford during the 1930s. For that, and his pioneering work as a radio commentator on the sport, his name lives on through the annual award of the Lance Todd Trophy, which is presented to the outstanding player in the Challenge Cup final.

Joe Miller, who played on the outside of Lance Todd, was snapped up from the local Pemberton Rovers amateur club in 1906. The flying wingman scored a club record 47 tries in the 1908/09 Championship season, topping the Northern Union chart with 49 through the addition of two tries scored for England against Australia – played at Glasgow's Celtic Park! On Christmas Day 1908, he equalled Jenkins' record by scoring five tries in the 27-11 victory over Swinton at Central Park. He was capped just once for Great Britain – the First Test against the 1911/12 Australian touring side – but made 3 appearances for England and 7 for Lancashire. With Wigan, he scored 151 tries in 206 matches.

Wigan emerged as a force in 1908/09, winning their first Championship by defeating Oldham 7-3 in the final and securing the Lancashire Cup for a second time. From left to right, back row: S. Wood, W. Hargreaves, H. Bouchier (vice-chairman), A. Laing, John H. Prescott, William Counsell. Middle row: Jack Hesketh (trainer), S. Latham (treasurer), Jack Brown, Tom Whittaker, Howell Francis, Massa Johnston, Dick Ramsdale, Jimmy Blears, Walter Cheetham, Jack Barton, J. Henderson, George Taylor (secretary). Front row: Neddy Jones, Johnny Thomas, Joe Miller, Lance Todd (vice-captain), John Counsell (chairman), Jimmy Leytham (captain), Bert Jenkins, Fred Gleave, Jim Sharrock, Dr Monks (honorary surgeon). The trophies are, from left to right: Lancashire Cup, Rugby League Championship, Lancashire League Championship, West Lancashire League.

Charlie Seeling (left) and William 'Massa' Johnston came to Britain in 1905/06 with the New Zealand Rugby Union team. Seeling, a tough-tackling loose-forward, signed for Wigan in January 1910. Later that year, in November, he played twice for Lancashire alongside fellow countryman Lance Todd. He appeared 226 times for Wigan but was unlucky with honours, losing in finals of the Championship three times, the Challenge Cup twice and the Lancashire Cup twice, but winning the lattermost in 1912. His son, also named Charlie, played for Wigan in the 1930s. Johnston, at hooker, switched codes in New Zealand, returning to Britain as a member of their 1907 touring side. He signed for Wigan in 1908, appearing in 39 matches over two seasons, transferring to Warrington in 1910.

Available from the mid-1880s, Baines cards – produced by John Baines of Bradford – were sold in packets of six and are now highly collectable items. Printed in colour, all the clubs of that time – both rugby and association football – were included. Like most teams, Wigan had several cards dedicated to them, two examples of which are reproduced on this page, including one depicting half-back Billy Halliwell (below), whose Wigan career spanned both the Rugby Union and Northern Union eras.

A measure of Wigan's rise to power during this period is indicated by this postcard featuring the club's five tourists, selected for the first Northern Union (Rugby League) tour to Australasia in 1910. Surrounding Johnny Thomas (centre) are, from left to right, top: Bert Jenkins, Jimmy Leytham. Bottom: Jim Sharrock, Dick Ramsdale. Jenkins and Leytham – with 14 and 12 respectively – were the tourist's top try scorers. Full-back Sharrock made 5 of his 6 appearances for Great Britain on the tour.

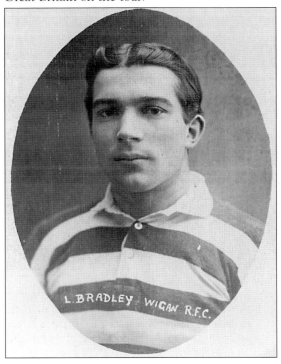

Wing three-quarter Lew Bradley came to Wigan from Pontypool Rugby Union Club at the start of the 1911/12 season. Although signed from the Principality, he was actually born in England and, effectively, replaced Jimmy Leytham, whose career ended in its prime due to injury. Bradley, who had great pace, registered 117 tries for Wigan in only 106 matches, including the only try for his team in the 1912 Championship final, which Huddersfield won 13-5. Later that year, he scored two in Wigan's fourth Lancashire Cup success, when Rochdale Hornets were vanquished 21-5 in the final. In March 1914, he equalled Leytham's club record by scoring six tries in the home match with Rochdale Hornets. The arrival of the First World War – which, sadly, was to cost him his life – restricted his time at the club to just four seasons.

The Wigan team in 1910/11. From left to right, back row: Fred Myers, James Shallcross, Dick Ramsdale, Charlie Seeling, Tom Whittaker, George Holding. Front row: Edmund Jones, Joe Miller, Lance Todd, Jimmy Leytham (captain), Jim Sharrock, Johnny Thomas, Bert Jenkins. It was to finish as a season of frustration for Wigan, being runners-up in both the Championship – to Oldham, for the second consecutive year – and Challenge Cup. The latter was the club's first appearance in the final, losing 4-0 to Broughton Rangers at Salford. Wigan lost out twice more in the Championship final during the next two seasons, on both occasions to Huddersfield's mighty side of that period – the so-called 'Team of All Talents'.

The 1911 Australian touring side played Wigan at Central Park on 28 October, losing 7-2, thanks to a well-taken try by Jimmy Leytham. It was the third time that they had beaten the Kangaroos, having met them twice during their first tour of 1908/09. In this picture, Australian tour captain and scrum-half Chris McKivat is about to feed a scrum. Wigan players are Johnny Thomas (left), Fred Gleave (at the base of the scrum) and Jim Sharrock (1) in the foreground.

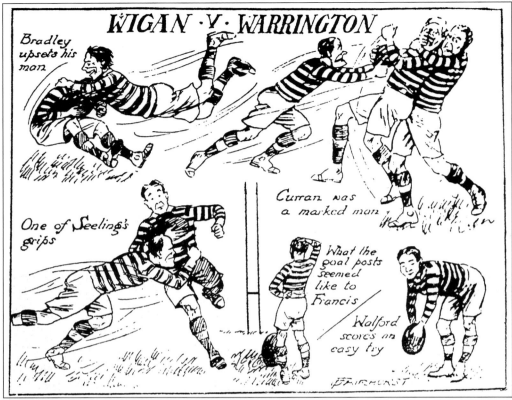

A cartoon strip, published in the *Wigan Examiner*, from the 1913/14 season featuring Wigan players Lew Bradley, William Curran, Arthur Francis, Charlie Seeling and Frank Walford. Curran and Francis had both arrived from New Zealand the previous season. The match was against Warrington at Central Park on 31 January, and won by Wigan 19-14.

Percy Coldrick had represented Wales at Rugby Union 6 times in the two seasons before his arrival from the Newport club in August 1912. Such was the impact of Coldrick, a quick-thinking and mobile forward, that he was included in the tour party to Australia and New Zealand in 1914. It was during the tour that he made his 4 appearances for Great Britain. He also represented Wales twice and the Other Nationalities team once. He played 280 times for Wigan and became captain of the side. This picture is from the Pinnace cigarette card series, referred to in the next chapter.

Two
Peerless Years
1921-1939

Throughout the history of Rugby League, there is not a player whose presence pervaded the club scene as much as Jim Sullivan's did at Wigan during the 1920s and '30s. With the First World War over and Wigan's wonderful side of the pre-war years virtually broken up, the Wigan public was looking for new heroes. The arrival of seventeen-year-old Sullivan in the summer of 1921 was the start of a dynasty that is without equal in the history of the sport, and his moniker of 'Peerless' was never more apt. This picture shows one of Sullivan's proudest moments when, as captain of the side, he takes centre-stage to display the Rugby League Challenge Cup, Wigan having won the first Wembley showpiece over Dewsbury in 1929.

Jim Sullivan joined Wigan in June 1921 from Cardiff Rugby Union Club. When he removed his Wigan jersey for the final time, he had amassed 774 appearances, 2,317 goals and 4,883 points for the club, and these figures are still unchallenged. He scored a club record of 161 goals in 1934/35 (a record that survived twenty-four years) and, including representative games, a Rugby League record 194 goals in 1933/34. On 14 February 1925, he landed 22 against amateurs Flimby & Fothergill in the Challenge Cup, which is still a Rugby League record. A tourist three times (1924, 1928 and 1932) and captain on the last occasion, he declined a history-making fourth trip, in 1936, for personal reasons. For twenty years, he dominated at full-back, repre-senting Great Britain (25 times), Wales (26), England (3), Other Nationalities (6), Glamorgan (1) and Glamorgan & Monmouthshire (12). Due to the Second World War, his last full season was 1939/40, although he played several times when peace resumed, the last at Batley in February 1946. The player-coach from 1932, he continued managing the Wigan team after retiring, creating one of the club's greatest sides before joining St Helens in 1952, overseeing their rise to power. He was an inductee to the Rugby League Hall of Fame in October 1988.

Danny Hurcombe, who could play half-back or centre, was one of the earliest signings made by Wigan after the First World War, arriving in November 1919 from Talywain Rugby Union Club. An elusive opponent, he quickly made his mark, completing his first season, that of 1919/20, by lining up for Wigan in the Challenge Cup final, followed by gaining a place in the 1920 tour party. History repeated itself in 1924, when Hurcombe again played in the Challenge Cup final for Wigan – the club's first success in that competition – before setting off on his second tour Down Under. Hurcombe earned 8 representative calls for Great Britain, 7 for Wales and 2 for Other Nationalities. He played 199 times for Wigan, before transferring to Halifax in 1926 for £600.

Danny Hurcombe, W.R.3.C.

yours Sincerely
John

J. Ring, WRFC.

Wing sensation Johnny Ring, signed in 1922, was another product from the Welsh Rugby Union conveyer belt, having registered 76 tries for Aberavon and represented Wales during 1920/21. In 331 appearances for Wigan, he scored an incredible total of 368 tries, including a club record of 7 in the Challenge Cup tie with Flimby & Fothergill in 1925 – a feat that he repeated twice more. His total of 62 tries in the 1925/26 seasons is still a club record. He toured in 1924, scoring 23 tries in 15 matches, representing Britain in the opening Test against Australia. He added a second, and final, appearance for Britain, against New Zealand in the First Test at Central Park, in 1926. He won 5 caps for Wales, 2 with Other Nationalities and 8 for the combined Glamorgan & Monmouthshire Counties team. In January 1932, after struggling to retain his first team place at Wigan, he transferred to Rochdale Hornets.

1921 · Wigan Rugby Football Team · 1922
Winners of the N.U. League Championship Cup.

Wigan regained the Rugby League Championship in 1921/22, after a gap of thirteen years, by defeating Oldham 13-2 in the final at Broughton, with nine Welshmen in their line-up. For captain Percy Coldrick (standing behind the Championship trophy) it was a proud moment, as he was one of the few survivors from the pre-war side, having joined Wigan ten years earlier.

LEAGUE COLOURS

B.D.V. CIGARETTES
WIGAN

From 1920 until 1922, BDV Cigarettes, manufactured by Godfrey Phillips Ltd, produced a series of 'silks' that featured twenty-seven Rugby League teams, in addition to covering Association Football and Rugby Union clubs. Produced in colour, the Wigan drawing naturally featured the famous cherry and white hoops.

Three famous Welshmen pose before a match in 1922. From left to right: Jim Sullivan, Jerry Shea and Johnny Ring. Centre three-quarter Shea joined Wigan from Newport in 1921, having represented Wales 4 times at Rugby Union, notably scoring 19 points against Scotland at Murrayfield in 1920. He played 85 times for Wigan over a three-year period, during which time he captained the side. A member of the victorious 1922 Championship team, he was later involved in the short-lived venture to establish a Rugby League club in Pontypridd during 1926/27. He was twice capped for Wales at Rugby League in 1922/23.

SOUTH AFRICAN PLAYERS AT WIGAN : : As Seen by Monk.

Above are impressions of the South African players now with the Wigan Rugby Club, at Central Park. Left to right: Van der Spuy, Van Rooyen, Burger, and Van Heerden.

Having long feasted on talent emerging from the valleys of South Wales, Wigan turned towards the South Africans during the mid-1920s – a period when six appeared in the first team at various times. Featured in this artist's impression are, from left to right: Constant van der Spuy (a stand-off who played twice for Wigan in 1924), George van Rooyen (second row forward, 178 matches between 1923-1928), Carl Burger (prop forward, 18 matches between 1924-1925) and Adrian 'Attie' van Heerden (wing three-quarter, 127 matches between 1923-1927). Except for van Rooyen, who arrived via Hull Kingston Rovers, all signed directly from South Africa's Simmer and Jack Rugby Union Club. Speedster van Heerden – scorer of 107 tries for Wigan – and van Rooyen shared in the club's Championship success of 1925/26 and Challenge Cup victory in 1924. The pair played twice for the South African Springboks in 1921 and represented the Other Nationalities Rugby League side in their 23-17 win over England at Headingley in October 1924. Van Heerden went to Leigh in 1927, whilst van Rooyen enjoyed further fame as a member of the Widnes team (whom he joined in 1929), upsetting the odds against St Helens at Wembley in 1930.

25

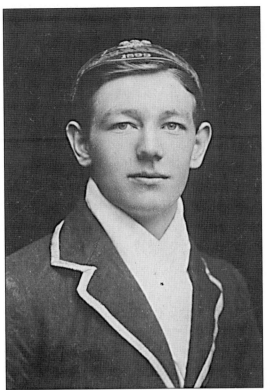

The Pinnace cigarette card series, first issued in 1923 by Godfrey Phillips Ltd, are now rare collector's items. The full set contained 2,462 cards, featuring players from Association Football, Rugby Union and Rugby League. Seventeen Wigan players were included, four of whom appear here. Sid Jerram joined Wigan in 1913, as part of a double signing that included his Swansea Rugby Union colleague and half-back partner George Owens. Almost nine years later, Jerram enjoyed his first major triumph as a member of the 1921/22 Championship-winning team that defeated Oldham in the final. He was in the Wigan side that lifted the Challenge Cup in 1924 and a member of the 1925/26 Championship-winning squad, a loss of form costing him a place in the final. He made 245 appearances for Wigan and represented Wales 6 times (partnering Owens on two occasions) and Other Nationalities twice.

Front row forward Tom Woods was another Welsh Rugby Union capture, signing from Pontypool in 1921. Although only appearing in 84 matches in three seasons, he played in the 1922 Championship final win and was a member of the 1922 Lancashire Cup-winning side. He was recognized by his selection for Wales against the 1921 Australian tourists at Pontypridd and twice against England during the 1922/23 season.

Local signing Bert Webster was a recruit from the grandly named Wigan Maoris team, making his debut in the Wigan pack in February 1918. The outstanding moment from his 128 appearances for Wigan came when he played in the club's first Challenge Cup final success in 1924, adding to the Lancashire Cup winners medal he received in 1922. Regarded as a speedy forward, he joined Bradford Northern in October 1924, where he became team captain but, tragically, his playing days ended when he passed away, suddenly, in 1926.

The Wigan career of Tom Coles was relatively brief, spanning just 66 matches from 1920 until 1923. Nonetheless, the former Ebbw Vale Rugby Union wingman contributed 47 tries to the Wigan cause and was in the team that secured the 1921/22 Championship title, when Oldham were defeated in the final at The Cliff, Broughton.

Wigan won the Rugby League Challenge Cup in 1924, with a convincing 21-4 win over their archrivals of the period, Oldham – a case of third time lucky after losing the 1911 and 1920 finals. Played at Rochdale, it attracted a record Challenge Cup final crowd of 41,831 that spilled onto the playing area, requiring mounted police to clear the field before the match started. From left to right, back row: J. McCarty (trainer), Percy Coldrick, Wilf Hodder, Fred Roffey, Sid Jerram (captain), George van Rooyen, John Hurst, Fred Brown, W. Fishwick. Front row: Attie van Heerden, Johnny Ring, George Owens, Tommy Parker, Tommy Howley, Jim Sullivan, Bert Webster, Harry Banks. Inset: Jack Price (left), Danny Hurcombe (right).

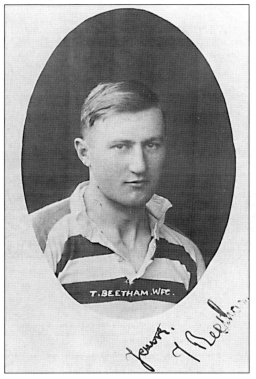

Prop forward Tommy Beetham was a signing from the Ambleside Rugby Union Club, making his debut against York at Central Park in September 1924. Over the next seven seasons, he appeared 262 times in the Wigan jersey, the most memorable occasions being the 1925/26 Championship final, when Warrington were defeated 22-10 at St Helens, and the historic 1929 Challenge Cup win over Dewsbury at Wembley. In September 1925, he was selected for Cumberland's County Championship fixture with Lancashire at Whitehaven, the first of 9 appearances.

THE HIGHFIELD "DERBY."

From 1922 until 1933, there were two professional clubs in Wigan, the other being the Pemberton-based Wigan Highfield. Wigan's visit normally came early in the campaign, no doubt to assist Highfield's cash flow. The match featured here took place on 27 September 1924, Wigan winning 24-10. The accompanying report stated: 'The visit of Wigan to Tunstall Lane stirred local rugby enthusiasts to such a degree, that it was regarded as a certainty that all records for attendance would easily be beaten. The previous record was 11,000 but on Saturday it is computed that the crowd easily numbered 16,000 so that the Highfield exchequer would receive a handsome fillip'.

New Zealand wingman Lou Brown, seen here racing down the right flank, joined Wigan in 1927, having scored 15 tries in 27 matches in the 1926/27 Kiwi tour of Britain. He was in Wigan's team at Wembley for the 1929 Challenge Cup final, scoring a try and, later that year, represented the Northern League XIII against the Australian tourists at Central Park. Further recognition came in 1930, when he played twice for Other Nationalities against England, scoring 5 tries. For Wigan, he crossed the line 106 times in 130 matches, before transferring to Halifax in October 1930, missing a second Wembley trip at the end of that season when the Yorkshire side suspended him for a breach of club discipline on the eve of the final.

A New Year greeting for 1925, featuring Wigan stars Attie van Heerden, Johnny Ring, Jim Sullivan, George van Rooyen, Danny Hurcombe and Tommy Beetham.

Lancashire Cup semi-final action, as Wigan take on Oldham at their Watersheddings ground. An unidentified Wigan player is tackled by three defenders, as Welsh prop Wilf Hodder (in hooped jersey) looks on. Played on 2 November 1925, the match was tied at 5-5. Wigan won the replay at Central Park nine days later by 52-3, but lost 15-11 in the final to Swinton.

Wilf Hodder fends off a tackle from Arthur Lloyd of Leeds at Headingley on 29 December 1928. Wigan won this contest 19-10.

The quarter-final round of the 1929 Rugby League Challenge Cup, as Jim Sullivan goes round a St Helens defender, with Wigan's Scottish centre Roy Kinnear – father of the comedy actor of the same name – looking on in the background. Played on 9 March at Knowsley Road in front of an attendance of 28,000, Wigan forced a 2-2 draw, winning the replay at Central Park 25-5 four days later, en route to reaching the inaugural Wembley final.

4 May 1929 – a proud day for Wigan and an historic day for Rugby League. The first Rugby League Challenge Cup final played at Wembley was Wigan's fourth appearance in the deciding tie.

Jim Sullivan leads his Wigan team out at Wembley in 1929. He was destined to score the first Rugby League points at the stadium with a 30-yard penalty goal in the third minute, when a Dewsbury player strayed offside.

Dewsbury prop Bill Rhodes is grounded by the Wigan defence in the 1929 Challenge Cup final. The Wembley scoreboard in the background shows Wigan 2-0 ahead, after Jim Sullivan's early penalty, a tally soon increased with the first of three tries in the fourteenth minute.

A beaming Jim Sullivan becomes the first Rugby League captain to walk down the steps from the royal box, after receiving the Challenge Cup following the 13-2 win over Dewsbury.

Rugby League Cup Souvenir.

PLAYED AT WEMBLEY,
MAY 4th, 1929.

J. SULLIVAN (CAPT.),
WIGAN.

A souvenir card to commemorate the 1929 Challenge Cup final, although the trophy illustrated appears to be the Lancashire Cup! Produced locally by the William Tickle Printing Works, it, almost inevitably, featured Jim Sullivan.

WIGAN FOOTBALL CLUB, LIMITED.

CENTRAL PARK,

DEAR SIR,   WIGAN,................................192*9*...

You have been selected against....*Dewsbury*..........

at....*Wembley*.......on Saturday next. The train leaves....*L & N W*.....

Station *4.20*... Kick-off.. *3.0*.. Training Tuesday and Thursday

Nights at 6-30. Players' Meeting, Thursday, 7-15.

Players receiving any injury must report same to me IN WRITING the day after the match, otherwise claims for insurance will not be recognised. This will be strictly enforced.   GEO. TAYLOR, Secretary.

Motor leaves Ground

Even the great Jim Sullivan could not rely on his place in the team! This postcard from club secretary George Taylor – sent to Sullivan's home address at Scholes in Wigan – advised him of his selection for the 1929 Challenge Cup final at Wembley! The card is date-stamped 29 April – just five days before the big game!

34

Sys Abram scored Wembley's first try, when he crossed the Dewsbury line in the fourteenth minute of the 1929 Challenge Cup final, after a spectacular 40-yard run. The former Salford stand-off half played 171 times for Wigan. He later captained Bramley, and is featured in that capacity in this cigarette card, part of a 1935 set called 'Football Club Captains' by Imperial Tobacco.

OGDEN'S CIGARETTES

S. ABRAM (BRAMLEY)

The less glamorous face of Rugby League, as halves Hector Gee (left) and George 'Darkie' Bennett train on a straw-covered pitch during a cold winter's day. The duo shared glory in the 1934 Championship final victory over Salford at Warrington. Bennett arrived at Central Park in 1930 from the Weston-Super-Mare Rugby Union Club and appeared 232 times for Wigan, joining Bradford Northern in 1937. Although born in England, he represented Wales 3 times during 1935 and 1936. Gee, an Australian Test scrum-half, arrived two years after Bennett, playing 353 matches before transferring to Leeds in 1944. He gained representative honours in Britain, when twice selected to oppose France with the Dominions XIII in 1936 and a British Empire XIII in 1937. The French connection continued in 1938, when he was included in a five-match tour of that country with the Northern Rugby League squad.

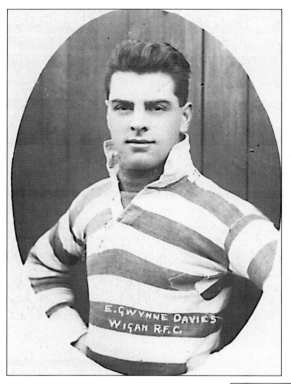

Gwynne Davies joined Wigan from Cheltenham Rugby Union Club in 1930. A centre with exceptional pace, he played 300 times for the club, during which time he registered 127 tries, including one in the 1934 Championship final win against Salford. In Rugby League, he represented his native Wales on 3 occasions and the combined Glamorgan & Monmouthshire side once, in the deciding match of the 1936/37 County Championship against Yorkshire at Halifax, which finished in favour of the White Rose team. Davies' biggest honour in the sport came with his inclusion in the 1936 touring side to the Antipodes, where he played 9 times, but missed out on Test selection.

Wing three-quarter Jack Morley was another former Wales Rugby Union international, having played 14 times for the Principality from 1929 until 1932, before transferring north from the Newport club. He also represented his country as a Rugby League player 5 times and appeared once for England, against Australia in Paris, during December 1933, in what was effectively a promotional match. He was included in the 1936 tour party Down Under, appearing in the First Test against Australia at the Sydney Cricket Ground. He made one further appearance for Britain in the opening test against the 1937 Kangaroos side at Headingley. He scored 223 tries in 292 matches with Wigan and was a member of the 1933/34 Championship team, scoring a try against Salford in the final.

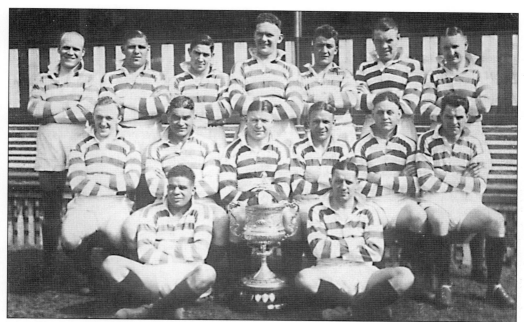

The Wigan line-up that captured the Championship Trophy in 1933/34, after defeating Salford 15-3 at Warrington in the final. From left to right, back row: Charlie Seeling (junior), Harold Edwards, Albert Davis, Bill Targett, Joe Golby, Reg Hathway, Ossie Griffiths. Middle row: Jack Morley, Len Mason, Jim Sullivan (captain), Dicky Twose, Joe Wilson, Gwynne Davies. Front row (on ground): George Bennett, Hector Gee. Following an eight-year gap since the previous success, it was the club's fourth title.

Len Mason was already a New Zealand Rugby League international when he was signed by Wigan in 1927, following the 1926/27 Kiwi tour of Britain. A tough second row forward, he appeared in 365 matches for Wigan, including the 1929 Wembley win over Dewsbury and the 1934 Championship final triumph over Salford, playing in the unaccustomed position of centre three-quarter in the latter. From 1929 to 1933, he represented the Other Nationalities 4 times and was twice picked for the Dominions XIII in 1936 and 1937, both games being against France. He joined Keighley in 1936 and was a member of their 1937 Wembley squad.

In 1934, Jean Galia – who had represented France Rugby Union 20 times – led a team of ex-Union players on a pioneering Rugby League tour of England under the label of 'France'. The six-match tour opened at Central Park on 10 March, when 8,000 spectators watched Wigan win 30-27. The two teams (with the Wigan players in their usual hooped jerseys) posed together for this historic photograph before the game. From left to right, back row: Jack Morley,

Charles Mathon, Joe Golby, Georges Blanc, Albert Davis, Francois Recaborde, Reg Hathway,
Robert Samatan, Bill Targett, Harold Edwards, Francois Nouel, Len Mason, Jean Duhau.
Middle row (seated): Gwynne Davies, Henri Dechavanne, George Bennett, Jean Galia, Jim
Sullivan, Maurice Porra, Hector Gee, Joseph Carrere, Billy Howarth, Antonin Barbazanges.
Front row (kneeling): Laurent Lambert, Jean Cassagneau, Dicky Twose.

The Wigan team, before meeting Broughton Rangers in their new home at Belle Vue Stadium, Manchester, on 5 January 1935, photographed on the speedway track surrounding the ground. From left to right, back row: Harold Edwards, Charlie Seeling (junior), Bill Targett, Gordon Innes, Joe Golby, Len Mason. Front row: Jack Morley, George Bennett, Hector Gee, Jim Sullivan (captain), Gwynne Davies, Alf Ellaby, Albert Davis. Wigan won this particular encounter 18-8.

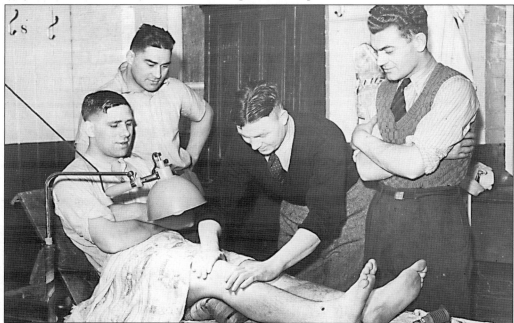

Harold Edwards relaxes on the treatment table, whilst player-coach Jim Sullivan works on his knee, watched by Len Mason (left) and Jimmy O'Sullivan. Edwards, a prop forward, made his Wigan debut in 1933 and played in 146 matches for the Cherry and Whites. In April 1935, he received his only representative honour, playing for Wales against England in a European Championship clash. O'Sullivan, an Irish wing three-quarter signed from Cork Institutional Rugby Union Club in 1936, played just 7 first-team matches for Wigan.

On 12 May 1934, Wigan defeated Warrington 32-19 at Dublin's Shelbourne Park ground, to win the first contest for the Irish Hospitals' Trust Challenge Trophy, watched by a crowd of 8,000 that included several hundred travelling Wigan fans. Having been fêted by the mayor of Dublin and the officials of the Trust in the evening, the Wigan players and club officials found themselves again being treated royally on their return to the borough two days later with the trophy, as Councillor J. Horne, the mayor of Wigan, hosted a reception at the Town Hall.

Twelve months later, Wigan sailed back across the Irish Sea to defend their prize against Leeds at Dalymount Park, Dublin. Wigan defeated Leeds 12-9 to retain the trophy in front of 7,000 spectators. The match itself was not considered to be the 'spectacle' provided the previous year with, according to the *Wigan Observer*, the 'hard sun-scorched ground evidently throwing players out of their stride'.

Rugby League Challenge Match, 1935

IRISH HOSPITALS' TRUST 100 GUINEA CHALLENGE TROPHY

JIM SULLIVAN, *Wigan Captain*

JIM BROUGH, *Leeds Captain*

At Dalymount Park, Dublin on Sunday, 12th May, 1935

WIGAN v LEEDS

Referee—MR. F. PEEL, Bradford.

Kick-off at 4 p.m. sharp by MR. JOSEPH McGRATH. Managing Director, Hospitals' Trust, Ltd.

1d ——— Official Programme ——— 1d

Jim Sullivan is reputed to have been featured in more cigarette card compilations than any other Rugby League player. Evidence for such a claim is indicated on this and the facing page. The card reproduced here was part of a set of fifty called 'Famous Rugby Players' and produced in monochrome by Imperial Tobacco in 1926/27.

A cigarette card from a set by John Player & Sons entitled 'Football Caricatures by Mac', Mac being a well-known cartoonist of the day. Containing fifty cards and printed in colour, they were introduced in September 1927.

The Imperial Tobacco set of 'Football Club Captains'
appeared in 1935 and contained fifty cards produced
in colour.

Another fifty-card set from the Imperial Tobacco
company, issued in 1935. They were produced in
colour and, aptly, called 'Football Caricatures'.

Lancashire County Rugby League
Challenge Cup

FINAL.

SALFORD v. WIGAN

Saturday, October 22nd, 1938,
ON
SWINTON GROUND,
STATION ROAD.

Kick-off - - 3-30 p.m.

PROGRAMME, ONE PENNY

The programme for the Lancashire Cup final versus Salford at Swinton's Station Road ground, played in October 1938. Wigan had found their opponents to be something of a bogey team during the decade, losing three consecutive County Cup finals to the Red Devils in 1934, 1935 and 1936. In 1938, Wigan reversed the trend by winning 10-7, thanks to five goals from the trusty boot of Jim Sullivan. It was Wigan's first win in the competition for ten years and their seventh overall.

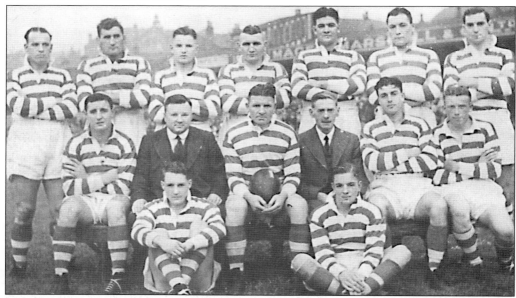

Wigan's team for the first home game of the 1939/40 season, against Hunslet on 30 August. From left to right, back row: Ossie Jones, Ike Jones, Joe Egan, George Banks, Percy Moxey, Eddie Watkins, Jack Bowen. Middle row: Ted Ward, Harry Sunderland (secretary/manager), Jim Sullivan (captain), Jim Entwistle (chairman), Denis Williamson, Johnny Lawrenson. Front row (on ground): Jim Jackson, Tommy Bradshaw. Four days after the match, which Wigan won 18-5, Britain and France declared war on Germany. Consequently, the fixture list was aborted and replaced by County Leagues. Sunderland, a former Australian tour manager and famous Rugby League journalist, was close to the end of his tenure at Wigan, staying less than a year. The picture is particularly interesting, as it includes youngsters Joe Egan, Ted Ward, Johnny Lawrenson and Tommy Bradshaw – players that would have a major impact at Central Park when peace returned.

Three
A Magnificent Seven
1940-1952

During the Second World War, Wigan was one of the few clubs in Lancashire able to continue. After heading the Lancashire League in 1940/41, they joined the Yorkshire clubs in a single competition, most of the west Pennine clubs having 'shut up shop'. Wigan won the wartime Championship for 1943/44, but lost to Bradford in that season's Challenge Cup final. Jim Sullivan, having retired as a player, concentrated on his coaching duties, moulding a team that would dominate the sport for the first seven post-war seasons. Wigan's rise was reflected at St Helens, and the traditional Boxing Day and Good Friday clashes were eagerly anticipated. The Good Friday meeting at Central Park in 1948, shown here, was the first between the two to attract over 40,000 spectators. Ken Gee is pictured passing to Joe Egan as the home side try to clear their line. Billy Blan (12) was a try scorer in Wigan's 22-11 win.

Versatile hooker Joe Egan signed from local junior Rugby League as a teenager in 1937, made his mark as one of the club's greatest ever captains in the post-war period, as Wigan dominated the sport. In 1948, he lifted the Challenge Cup at Wembley, bringing the prized trophy back to the borough for the first time in nineteen years. He was included in the tour party to Australia and New Zealand in 1946 and 1950, appearing 14 times for Great Britain. He also represented England (21 matches) and Lancashire (10). His 362 games for Wigan included two Championship final wins (a figure that would have doubled, had he not had to set sail on those two tours) and five Lancashire Cup victories. He later played and coached at Leigh, returning in the latter capacity to Wigan from 1956 to 1961, playing a key part in the club's renaissance.

Ken Gee, at open-side prop, created, with Egan, the platform upon which the great Wigan team of the period was built. The two names are inextricably linked whenever conversation turns to that period in the club's history. Signed in 1933, Gee began to feature in the team before the outbreak of the Second World War, firmly establishing his place in the post-war period. He joined Egan on the 1946 and 1950 tours and represented Great Britain (18 appearances), England (20) and Lancashire (12). He played a mammoth 559 times for Wigan – second only to Jim Sullivan – and kicked 508 goals. He was a Wembley winner in 1948 and 1951, and shared in three Championship final wins but, like Egan, missed another two due to tour commitments. He also won Lancashire Cup winners' medals an incredible seven times.

Another 1946 tourist, Ted Ward was a classy Welsh centre three-quarter who came from Llanelli in 1938 and played 213 times for Wigan. Effectively taking over the kicking duties from Jim Sullivan, he accumulated 480 goals to add to his 57 tries. After missing the 1946 Championship final win, due to being on board the *Indomitable* as it headed Down Under for the first post-war tour, he was in the successful line-ups of 1947 and 1950 and a winner at Wembley in 1948. He played for Great Britain 3 times and Wales 13. After joining the short-lived Cardiff venture in 1951, he returned to Central Park in 1953 as coach for a three-year period.

Ernie Ashcroft is one of the finest centres in the history of the Wigan club. He played in 530 matches scoring 241 tries, his lengthy playing career covering the years 1942 until 1958. He was a tourist twice – in 1950 and 1954 – and was recognized by Great Britain (11 caps), England (11) and Lancashire (10). After receiving a losers' medal in Wembley's first post-war final, he was in the side that defeated Bradford Northern at the stadium in 1948. A Championship winner in 1944, 1946 and 1947, he missed the 1950 final due to the tour. He also played in eight Lancashire Cup finals for Wigan, winning in five. In 1958, he joined Huddersfield.

Wigan hooker Jack Blan attempts to force his way through the Wakefield Trinity defence in the 1946 Challenge Cup final at Wembley. Wigan were handicapped by the absence of Joe Egan, Ken Gee, Martin Ryan and Ted Ward, en route Down Under, but only lost 13-12 after Billy Stott's sensational late penalty goal for Trinity. Consolation came two weeks later, when Wigan became the first post-war Champions by defeating Huddersfield 13-4 at Maine Road, Manchester.

A unique moment, as Wigan and Wakefield pose together at the Yorkshire club's Belle Vue ground on 4 January 1947, the two holding all six major trophies. From left to right, back row: Denis Baddeley, Jim Higgins, Mick Exley, Albany Longley, Len Marson, Jack Booth, Derek Howes (all Wakefield), Jack Blan (Wigan), Len Bratley (Wakefield), Harry Atkinson, Billy Blan, Joe Shovelton, Gordon Ratcliffe, Johnny Lawrenson, George Banks, Ted Ward, George Woosey (all Wigan). Front row (kneeling): Ken Brooks, Billy Banks, Jack Perry, Billy Stott, Harry Wilkinson, Billy Teall (all Wakefield), Jack Cunliffe, Cec Mountford, Ted Toohey, Brian Nordgren (all Wigan). The trophies, from left to right, are: Lancashire Challenge Cup, Lancashire League Championship, Rugby League Championship, Rugby League Challenge Cup, Yorkshire League Championship, Yorkshire Challenge Cup. Ernie Ashcroft, Tommy Bradshaw, Joe Egan, Ken Gee and Martin Ryan were rested for this match, won 8-7 by Wakefield, avenging a New Year's Day defeat at Central Park.

Within days of winning the 1946 Lancashire Cup final against Belle Vue Rangers, Wigan headed across the channel for a short tour of France. On 1 November, they met the Perpignan-based Catalan team, winning 37-8 (with an attendance of 8,000) and, two days later, played French Champions Carcasonne, registering a 26-14 victory (10,000). The trip had its poignant moments, with wreaths being laid in memory of those who had fallen in the Second World War. Here, we see coach Wigan Jim Sullivan (left), who kicked off the second game, during a break in one of the encounters, with, from left to right: George Banks, Martin Ryan, Jack Blan (obscured behind Ryan), Ernie Ashcroft (at the back), Tommy Bradshaw, Ken Gee, Johnny Lawrenson, Ted Ward and Billy Blan.

Joe Egan leads the team out from the Central Park Pavilion, followed by George Banks, Jack Blan and Martin Ryan. Taken on 28 December 1946, Wigan subsequently defeated visitors Barrow 10-3.

The (Jimmy) Leytham/(Bert) Jenkins Memorial Scoreboard, first used for the match with Swinton on 13 September 1947 (which Wigan won 50-12), was, literally, ahead of its time. It incorporated a clock, and enabled the opposing team to be named, rather than the usual practice of being referred to as 'visitors'. It also allowed other half-time scores to be displayed. The clock, although not operational for the Swinton fixture, was put in place on the morning of the match. The Wigan v. Castleford game, indicated on the scoreboard, took place on 7 February 1948, and was a Challenge Cup first round, first leg tie. Wigan won 27-0, taking the second leg seven days later 19-7, on the way to winning the cup.

Further ground embellishment came in 1950, with the addition of perimeter 'ringside' seats, increasing the capacity by a further 500. First used at the England v. Wales international on 1 March, and an exciting venture in its day, it would be outlawed in these safety-conscious times, when spectators are kept strictly behind barriers.

Martin Ryan, seen here placing the ball for a kick at goal, was a full-back ahead of his time. Whilst most of his ilk were happy to stand patiently behind their colleagues and defend the citadel, Ryan was providing attacking options by linking up with his three-quarters. Signed after the outbreak of war, in 1940, he took his place on the Great Britain tour to the Antipodes in 1946, repeating that honour four years later. Apart from 4 appearances for Great Britain, he played for England 12 times and Lancashire 9. He was in the Wigan sides that won the Challenge Cup final in 1948 and the Championship final of 1952. In 1944, he was at stand-off in the wartime Championship decider, when Dewsbury were beaten. He played 300 times for Wigan, scoring 67 tries and 63 goals.

Front row forward George Banks was one of the unsung heroes of the Wigan team before and immediately after the Second World War. Neither a tourist, nor even rising to the heights of county representation, he still claimed 246 appearances in the Wigan colours. He made his senior debut with Dewsbury in 1931, joined London-based Streatham and Mitcham in 1935, and then Wigan in 1936. Honours came late in his career; he was thirty-seven when he appeared in the side that narrowly lost to Wakefield at Wembley in 1946, gaining consolation in the victorious Championship final teams of 1946 and 1947, against Huddersfield and Dewsbury respectively.

Three-quarter Johnny Lawrenson was a local Rugby Union signing in 1938, enjoying a distinguished career at Wigan. Scoring 187 tries and 128 goals in 219 appearances, his try count was impressive, as he played mostly in the centre. He was a winner in the 1944 and 1947 Championship finals, but was unlucky in missing Wembley twice; in 1946 and 1948 (the former due to army duties, the latter through injury). His move to Workington Town in 1949 gave him the opportunity to make amends, and he scored two tries in the 1952 Challenge Cup final, helping the Cumbrians vanquish Featherstone Rovers. He also touched down for Town in their impressive Championship final victory over Warrington in 1951. Although overlooked for a tour place, he played in all three Tests against the 1948/49 Kangaroos, scoring two vital tries in the second match at Swinton to win the series, and represented England 10 times and Lancashire 7.

Two of the greatest New Zealanders to appear for Wigan were Brian Nordgren (left) and Cec Mountford. Nordgren, a wingman with tremendous pace, arrived from his native land during the 1945/46 season and, within months, appeared at Wembley against Wakefield Trinity. Despite scoring two tries, he found himself on the losing side 13-12. For Nordgren, it was a traumatic experience, missing all seven of his kicks at goal. Two weeks later, however, he savoured the first of four Championship final successes when Huddersfield were defeated 13-4 at Maine Road and, after missing the 1948 Challenge Cup final, tasted Wembley glory in 1951. A few months after Nordgren's arrival, Mountford's signature was obtained, the stand-off becoming one of the most exciting out-halves to appear in Britain from the land of the Kiwi. He

featured in the Championship final wins of 1947 and 1950, and was a Wembley winner in 1948 and 1951, the latter as team captain and first overseas player to claim the Lance Todd Trophy. That was also his final match for Wigan, as he moved on to become a successful coach at Warrington. Nordgren played for Wigan 294 times, scoring 312 tries, including 57 in 1949/50, whilst Mountford appeared on 210 occasions. Both represented the Other Nationalities side.

Local Rugby Union discovery Gordon Ratcliffe was a wingman who blossomed at Wigan under the influence of coach Jim Sullivan. He played in the Challenge Cup final at Wembley in 1946 and 1948 and was a winner in the 1946 Championship final. He appeared in six Lancashire Cup finals, finishing on top in five of them. He was included in the 1950 tour party, where he played in two of the Test matches against Australia, adding to his previous outing against New Zealand at Headingley in 1947. He made 4 appearances for England and 3 for Lancashire. In 212 matches for Wigan, he scored 185 tries and, in August 1947, equalled Johnny Ring's record of seven in a match, against Liverpool Stanley at Central Park.

Tense action from Batley's Mount Pleasant ground on 26 April 1947. Tommy Bradshaw makes a break round the blind side of the scrum with the try line only yards away, watched closely by loose forward Jack Blan (on his immediate right). The match produced a gritty performance from mid-table Batley, who lost narrowly to the League leaders 6-5.

Wigan entertained Workington Town – in only their second season – at a packed Central Park on 26 May 1947. Centre Ted Ward lands a successful goal kick from in front of the posts, helping his side to an 18-6 win. The season was running late due to a winter freeze-up through February and March.

The atrocious winter weather meant that the 1946/47 Championship final did not take place until 21 June, when Wigan faced Dewsbury. The Yorkshire side's captain and scrum-half, Harry Royal, gets the ball away from the scrum to his stand-off, Cyril Gilbertson. Wigan loose forward Jack Blan (right) watches intently.

Wigan leave the Maine Road pitch at Manchester in triumph after the 1947 Championship final, and captain Joe Egan is 'chaired' from the field. Wigan had won 13-4 to retain the Championship, having beaten Huddersfield by an identical score at the same ground in the climax to the previous season.

The 1946/47 Wigan team. Coach Jim Sullivan (middle row, extreme right) and club officials join the players to show off their latest collection of silverware. The players are, from left to right, middle row: Ernie Ashcroft, Ted Ward, Brian Nordgren, Martin Ryan, Harry Atkinson, Gordon Ratcliffe, Johnny Lawrenson, Jack Hilton, Frank Barton, George Banks. Front row

(seated): Billy Blan, Ken Gee, Tommy Bradshaw, Joe Egan (captain), Cec Mountford, Jack Blan, Reg Lowrey, Jack Cunliffe. The trophies on show are, from left to right: Rugby League Championship, Lancashire League Championship, Wardonia Cup, Lancashire Challenge Cup. The Wardonia Cup was contested annually with Warrington as a pre-season charity match.

Wigan and the French Champions of the previous two seasons, Carcasonne, captained by the legendary Puig Aubert, line up on a frozen pitch before their friendly at Central Park on Wednesday 12 March 1947. In the midst of a terrible winter, the ground was treated with antifreeze to make it playable, but a heavy snowfall during the match created difficult conditions. Due to a fixture backlog, Wigan had a Challenge Cup tie with Featherstone Rovers the next day, followed by a League fixture with Widnes two days after that! It was, therefore, not surprising that Wigan rested several players, aiding the visitors in causing an upset by winning 11-8. The attendance was 10,000.

On 12 May 1948, the newly crowned French champions, Roanne (who had deposed Carcasonne 3-2 in their domestic final) visited Central Park. Watched by a bumper 24,000 crowd, the teams are being led out by the Roanne president, Monsieur Deveroix (left), and Wigan chairman, Harry Platt, who is followed by his team captain, Joe Egan. For once, the scoreboard was found wanting, with the opposition being labelled as 'France'. Wigan won 17-15.

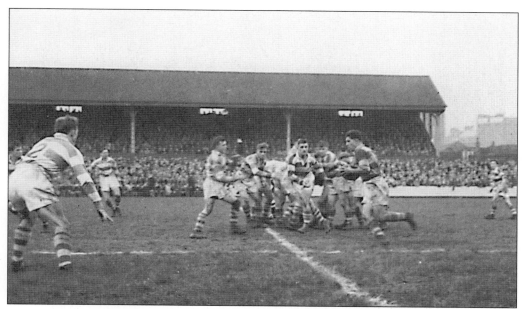

Action from the 1947 Lancashire Cup final against Belle Vue Rangers at Warrington. Wigan second row Les White (centre of picture) is about to halt a Belle Vue raid, with Gordon Ratcliffe (2) on the left. Played on 1 November, Wigan won 10-7, thanks to a try each from Ratcliffe and Brian Nordgren. Wigan retained the cup, having beaten the Rangers twelve months earlier by 9-3 in the decider at Swinton. Over the next few years, Wigan kept a firm grip on the trophy, winning it on six consecutive occasions between 1946 and 1951.

A scene from the 1948 Challenge Cup semi-final match against Rochdale Hornets, as Ted Ward places the ball near the touch-line before attempting to convert a Wigan try. The match took place on 3 April at Station Road, Swinton, the Cherry and Whites winning 11-0.

RUGBY LEAGUE CHALLENGE CUP

FINAL TIE

BRADFORD NORTHERN v WIGAN
SOUVENIR PROGRAMME • ONE SHILLING

WEMBLEY EMPIRE STADIUM

Chairman and Managing Director: Sir ARTHUR J. ELVIN M.B.E.

SAT. MAY 1st. 1948. KICK-OFF 3 P.M

Wigan reached their seventh Challenge Cup final – and third at Wembley – in 1948, seeking a third win after successes in 1924 and 1929. Having lost at Wembley in 1946, when the team was handicapped by the absence of four tourists, there was a confident feeling in the Wigan camp that this could be their year, even though Bradford had unexpectedly defeated them 15-3 in the previous week's Championship semi-final at Central Park.

Bradford Northern second row man Trevor Foster tackles Wigan full-back Martin Ryan during the 1948 final at Wembley. A tense match, watched by a record 91,465 crowd, was settled in the final minutes, when Wigan prop Frank Barton touched down, making it 8-3 for The Colliers, as they were referred to at that time. Back row forward Bill Hudson, looking on in the background, arrived at Wigan in 1947 from Batley for a Rugby League record of £2,000. He was selected by Great Britain for the Third Test at Odsal against Australia in 1949.

Wigan went back to Wembley, for the third time in six post-war finals, in 1951. The match, watched by 94,262 spectators, took place in wet and muddy conditions, rather than under the blue skies that normally accompanied the big day.

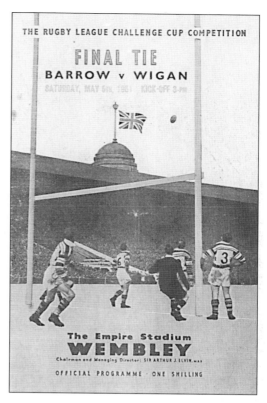

The victorious Wigan team hold New Zealand captain Cec Mountford aloft after grinding out a 10-0 win over Barrow in an unspectacular final which was spoilt by the poor conditions.

Wigan winger – and future chairman – Jack Hilton, leaves Swinton's Ken Birkett (5) floun-dering, as he races away supported by Frank Barton and Billy Blan (right). Wigan won this home fixture 39-17 on 11 September 1948.

The 1948 Australian touring side met Wigan on 20 October. It was their eighth meeting and Wigan kept up an excellent record by winning for the fourth time, 16-11. Wigan centre Ernie Ashcroft is pictured attempting to halt a pass to the Australian flank. Frank Barton (left) and Cec Mountford are covering with Ted Ward (right) looking on in the background.

A proud day for the borough! Five Wigan-born players before the Third Test against Australia at Odsal Stadium, Bradford, on 29 January 1949. From left to right: Joe Egan, Martin Ryan, Johnny Lawrenson, Ken Gee and George Curran. Front row forward Curran of Salford, was the only player in the group not attached to the Wigan club at the time, but joined his home town team the following year and featured in the 1951 win over Barrow at Wembley.

Tommy Bradshaw, seen here with the coveted Rugby League Challenge Cup, was one of the most outstanding and gifted scrum-halves in the history of the club. Signed locally in 1939, he made his mark in the post-war years and played in 302 matches for Wigan. His talent was recognized by a place on the 1950 tour, in which he made 4 of his 6 appearances for Great Britain. He also represented England 14 times and Lancashire 3. He took part in the Championship final victories of 1944, 1946 and 1947, and appeared at Wembley three times (1946, 1948 and 1951), winning on all but the first occasion. In January 1952, he joined Leigh.

Loose-forward Billy Blan joined his brother, Jack, at Wigan in 1945 and played in 255 matches for the club. That total covered three successful Championship finals – including the historic 1950 decider when he scored a try – and all three Challenge Cup finals at Wembley during the period. He represented Great Britain in all three Tests against the 1951 Kiwi side and, during a three-season spell (from 1950/51 onwards), appeared 3 times for England and 6 for Lancashire. He transferred to Leeds in the summer of 1953, and in January 1955, he joined his former mentor Jim Sullivan at St Helens.

'Tough as teak' forward Frank Barton was another Wigan post-war star who first broke into the side during the Second World War. Signed in 1940, his first match was at home to Hull in September 1941, playing blind-side prop and partnering Ken Gee and Joe Egan in the front row. The three dominated opposing packs for years to come, although much of Barton's career at Wigan was destined for the second row. He appeared for Wigan in three successful Championship finals (1946, 1947, 1950) and was in three Wembley sides (1946, 1948, 1951). Towards the end of his Central Park career in 1951/52, he played twice for Great Britain, against New Zealand and France. After 279 matches, he joined Barrow in 1953, reaching his fourth Wembley final in 1955, a 21-12 victory over Workington Town. He was capped twice each by England and Lancashire.

Widnesian centre Jack Broome made the first of 215 Wigan appearances at home to Halifax in April 1949, having signed in 1948. His biggest day in the cherry-and-white colours was undoubtedly at Wembley in 1951 when, with the score finely balanced at 2-0 in Wigan's favour, he played a key part in the move that sent wing partner Jack Hilton racing in during the 59th minute to break the deadlock. He also appeared in the Championship-winning sides for the 1950 and 1952 finals. In May 1951, he represented Great Britain against Australasia in a special match staged at Headingley, as part of the Festival of Britain celebrations. He appeared twice in European Championship fixtures for England in 1950, and was selected 6 times for Lancashire.

A wonderful accolade for the Wigan club, with a record eight players selected for the 1950 tour to Australia and New Zealand. From left to right, back row: Gordon Ratcliffe, Jack Cunliffe, Joe Egan, Jack Hilton, Ernie Ashcroft. Front row: Martin Ryan, Tommy Bradshaw, Ken Gee. Seven of them (the exception was Cunliffe, who later played in one of the New Zealand Tests) appeared together for the First Test in Sydney, when Australia were defeated 6-4, courtesy of two Hilton tries.

The programme for the 1950 Championship final, played at Manchester City Football Club's Maine Road ground on 13 May. As in 1946, the early departure of the tourists, who had set sail in mid-April, meant Wigan had to participate in a major final with a depleted team. Forced to enter the field without eight of their star performers, it is remembered as the club's 'finest hour'.

Nat Silcock scores against Huddersfield in the 1950 Championship final. It was a try that, effectively, ended the challenge of the Fartowners, as Wigan pulled off a sensational 20-2 victory, watched by a 65,065-strong crowd. Silcock, drafted on the wing in the absence of tourists Gordon Ratcliffe and Jack Hilton, normally played in the second row. He had his turn Down Under, when included in the 1954 tour. He was in the Wigan side that beat Barrow at Wembley in 1951 and transferred to St Helens in 1955.

Jack Cunliffe was a local signing in 1939, whilst still a teenager. Essentially a full-back, he competed for that role with, firstly, Martin Ryan and, latterly, Don Platt, playing many of his games in the three-quarter line. In spite of that, he appeared in 447 matches for Wigan. He was at full-back in the 1946 and 1947 Championship final wins and took part in a third triumph in 1952, when he played at stand-off. After being on the losing side in the 1946 Challenge Cup final at Wembley, he returned as a winner in 1951 and 1958. His consistency was recognized by selection for both the 1950 and 1954 tour parties. He played in 4 matches for Great Britain and gained 7 caps each for England and Lancashire.

In 1950, it looked as though Italy was going to follow the French example and spread Rugby League deeper into the European continent. A pioneering Italian touring side visited England and Wales in August and September for six matches, meeting Wigan in the first of those on 26 August. A twenty-one team Italian league developed soon after, but faded by the end of the decade due to the lack of government support. Our picture shows Nat Silcock touching down, supported by Jack Broome (right). Wigan won 49-28, watched by a 14,000 crowd. The old 'Dutch Barn' that dominates the background was built in 1911, being replaced in 1954 by the Popular Side Stand.

A unique photograph from 1950 that shows the view seen by many a beaten defence, as George Roughley heads for the try line, supported by Brian Nordgren (5). Wigan went on to win this match, against Huddersfield at Central Park on 9 September, 48-13. Roughley, who played in the 1951 win over Barrow at Wembley, joined Huddersfield in December 1954, having spent a year with Salford.

Wigan's Nat Silcock leaves a Leeds defender trailing as he beats the cover. Playing at Headingley on 16 Sepember 1950, Wigan beat Leeds 23-12, despite the fact that they were still awaiting the return of their 1950 tourists.

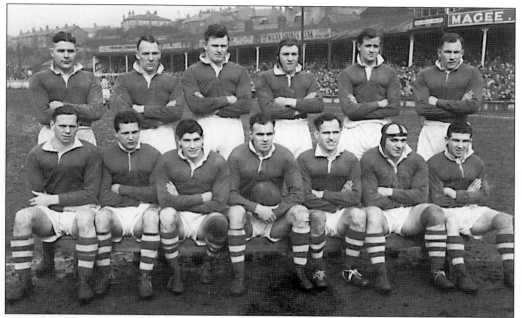

The Wigan team that entertained Dewsbury on 31 March 1951. From left to right, back row: Frank Barton, George Curran, Nat Silcock, Jack Large, Gordon Ratcliffe, Brian Nordgren. Front row: Ernie Ashcroft, George Roughley, Jack Broome, Billy Blan, Jack Cunliffe, Ken Gee, Johnny Alty. Wigan won the subsequent encounter 12-2.

The 1952 Championship semi-final against Hull at Central Park on 3 May. Left-winger Brian Nordgren powers over the line to register his hat-trick in a tight game, as Wigan squeezed out Hull 13-9.

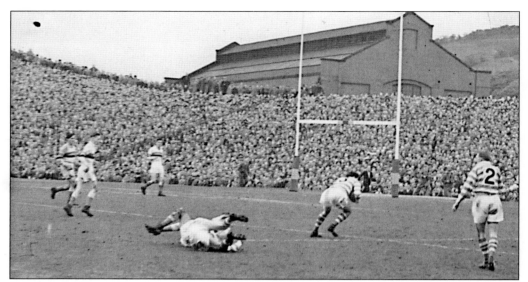

Centre Jack Broome heads for the try line, supported by right-wing partner Jack Hilton (2), in the 1952 Championship final against Bradford Northern at Leeds Road, home to Huddersfield Town Football Club, on 10 May. A try was not forthcoming on this occasion, but Wigan ran out winners 13-6 to claim their ninth Championship (and fourth since the Second World War).

Celebration time, as Wigan captain Jack Cunliffe holds up the Championship trophy, supported by his colleagues, after the 1952 final. From left to right: Brian Nordgren, Ronnie Mather, Jack Large (at back), Jack Hilton, Ken Gee (at back), George Roughley, Cunliffe (holding trophy), Harry Street, Johnny Alty, Martin Ryan, Jack Broome, George Woosey, Nat Silcock. This match signalled the end of an era for Wigan. Jim Sullivan took over the reins at St Helens a month later, ending a thirty-one-year association with Wigan, the last twenty as player-coach and coach. The next piece of silverware would not arrive in the Wigan boardroom until 1958.

Four
The Wembley Wizards
1953-1967

After the break-up of the all-conquering side of the immediate post-war period, Wigan fans waited six years until 1958 before success returned. One chink of sunlight in a cloudy sky was the much-heralded arrival of Billy Boston in 1953, an event that kept the Central Park turnstiles clicking while team-building took its course. Wigan bounced back spectacularly under new coach and former player Joe Egan, dominating the Challenge Cup as no club had before. This 1966 line-up, which took Wigan to Wembley for the sixth time in nine seasons, met Widnes in a Championship semi-final at Central Park on 30 April. From left to right, back row: Laurie Gilfedder, Danny Gardiner, Geoff Lyon, Tom Woosey, Billy Boston, Brian McTigue, Tony Stephens. Middle row (seated): Chris Hesketh, David Stephens, Trevor Lake, Eric Ashton (captain), Ray Ashby, Colin Clarke, Harry Major. Front row (kneeling): Cliff Hill, Frank Parr. Clarke missed the final through suspension.

Wigan's six Wembley finals of the period are synonymous with the names of Billy Boston (left), Eric Ashton (centre) and Brian McTigue. The three men, seen at the famous stadium on the eve of another Wembley showpiece, appeared in all of them, setting a record not surpassed until the Widnes trio of Mick Adams, Keith Elwell and Eric Hughes made it seven in 1984 – against Wigan! Ashton was captain in all six finals – still a Rugby League record – and player-coach in two of them, whilst McTigue took the prestigious Lance Todd Trophy award in 1959. Boston scored just two tries at Wembley, both in the 1959 final, a low return for the most prolific try scorer the club has ever known, although he did play out of position – at centre – in the 1958 contest.

A unique pre-match moment, as a Blackpool Borough supporter presents a stick of the town's famous rock to Wigan captain Ernie Ashcroft. It was to mark the seaside club's first appearance at Central Park on 23 October 1954, after their recent admittance to the Rugby Football League. Wigan won 39-2, with a young Billy Boston claiming a hat-trick of tries against the club he would conclude his career with some fifteen years later.

Although it was a barren spell for the Wigan trophy cabinet, the club contributed four players to the tour of Australia and New Zealand in 1954. From left to right: Billy Boston, Nat Silcock, Jack Cunliffe and Ernie Ashcroft. Having made his senior debut for Wigan in November 1953, Boston left Britain with just 9 first-team games under his belt. Still only nineteen, he was to be a sensation, scoring a tour record 36 tries – achieved in only 18 matches – equalling Great Britain's Test Match record with four touchdowns against New Zealand in Auckland.

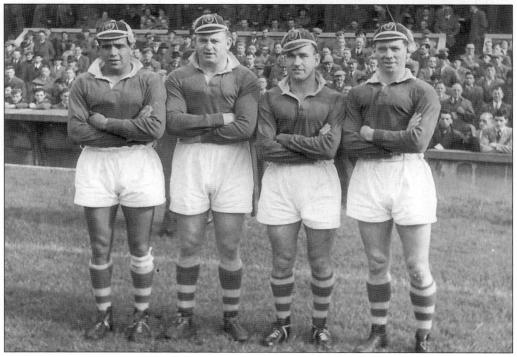

Here, we recall the magic of the great Billy Boston, whose charging runs down the right flank brought the Central Park crowd to its feet time after time during his fifteen seasons with Wigan. His arrival in 1953 created unprecedented interest and his debut, for the reserves against Barrow on 31 October 1953, attracted 8,500 spectators to Central Park. Boston is pictured here before that much-heralded first outing for the 'A' team.

Boston adds to his tally against Barrow at Central Park on 28 September 1957. Despite playing at stand-off in this match, he still managed to score a hat-trick, helping Wigan to a 48-5 win. He scored three tries or more in 51 matches for Wigan, including seven on two occasions – a club record he shared with Johnny Ring and Gordon Ratcliffe at the time.

Another positional change for Boston, but still the tries keep coming! A rare appearance in the second row came in the home match with Halifax on 20 August 1966. On this occasion, the visitors won 34-22.

Typical Boston! Always well-marked and surrounded by defenders, the outcome was usually the same – another try for the Boston inventory! His final career total of 571 included a club record 478 for Wigan in 487 appearances. His highest single season return for the club was 54 in 1958/59.

Powerhouse prop John Barton spent two seasons at Leigh under coach Joe Egan, following him to Wigan in 1956. With hookers Bill Sayer and Brian McTigue, he contributed to a formidable front row that took Wigan to Wembley in 1958, 1961 and 1963. The three also appeared together in the 1959 final, when McTigue was in the second row, Bill Bretherton being selected at prop. Barton was also a winner in the 1960 Championship final over Wakefield Trinity, a match played at Odsal Stadium in front of a massive 83,000 crowd. Barton played 278 times for Wigan and represented Great Britain on 2 occasions and Lancashire on 11.

Frank Collier was another mighty Wigan forward of the era, whose ball distribution skills belied his bulky frame. He signed for his hometown club in 1951 and was to play 323 matches for the Cherry and Whites. He joined Widnes in 1964 and, later that year, won the Lance Todd Trophy at Wembley as the Chemics defeated Hull Kingston Rovers. That was his fourth visit to the stadium, following a win with Wigan in 1958 and two defeats (1961 and 1963). He was at blind-side prop in the memorable Championship final win over Wakefield Trinity in 1960. Having earned 9 caps for Lancashire (from 1958 to 1962), he finally gained international recognition when he played for Great Britain in the Third Test against Australia at Headingley in November 1963. Four months later, following his move to Widnes, he made his second and final appearance, against France in Perpignan.

David Bolton – seen here in Wigan's change strip, about to score a try – was one of the most exciting stand-off halves in the history of the club. The 300 appearances he would make for his local team began in 1954, shortly after he was signed as a seventeen-year-old. Selected 23 times for Great Britain, he was a tourist in 1958 and 1962, breaking his collarbone in the infamous Second Test against Australia in the former tour when Britain won with an injury-ravaged side. He was in the Wigan team that took the 1960 Championship final and made four Challenge Cup final appearances at Wembley. Capped 7 times for Lancashire, he left Wigan in 1964 and headed for Australia.

Rhodesian full-back Fred Griffiths – who arrived at Central Park in 1957 with the curious nickname of 'Punchy' – made quite an impact at Wigan during his five-year stay. In 1958/59, he set a new club record with 176 goals and came close to bettering that with 174 three years later. His aggregate of 663 goals included valuable contributions of six in both the 1959 Wembley win over Hull and the 1960 Championship clincher with Wakefield Trinity at Odsal Stadium. His three penalty goals in the 1961 Challenge Cup final against St Helens were his side's only points in a disappointing 12-6 defeat. In 1962, his contract at Central Park concluded, he went to Australia to join the North Sydney Club.

EAST
STANDING
ENCLOSURE

ENTER AT TURNSTILES
(See plan & conditions on back)

ENTRANCE

C
14

EMPIRE STADIUM, WEMBLEY
RUGBY LEAGUE
FINAL
SATURDAY, MAY 10th, 1958
KICK-OFF 3 p.m.

Price 3/-   *Bracewell Smith*
Chairman,
Wembley Stadium Limited
THIS PORTION TO BE RETAINED
This Ticket is issued on the condition that
it is not re-sold for more than its face value

The start of the great Wembley adventure. A ticket for the 1958 Wigan *v.* Workington Town final, costing 3 shillings (15 pence) for the East Standing Enclosure, situated behind the goals.

The Wigan team before meeting St Helens at Knowsley Road on Good Friday, 4 April 1958 (lost 32-7). From left to right, back row: John Barton, Bill Sayer, Brian McTigue, Frank Collier, Norman Cherrington, Ernie Ashcroft, Roy Evans. Front row: Rees Thomas, Mick Sullivan, Eric Ashton (captain), David Bolton, Jack Cunliffe, Billy Boston. Wigan had beaten a determined Rochdale Hornets side 5-3 in the previous weekend's semi-final at Swinton to reach Wembley for the first time since 1951. From the above line-up, Ashcroft (rib injury) and Evans (influenza) were unable take their places at Wembley, and were replaced by Terry O'Grady and Bernard McGurrin.

Bernard McGurrin attempts to outwit Workington's John O'Neill (left) and Ike Southward in the 1958 Challenge Cup final at Wembley. Southward scored all of his side's points, but it was to no avail, as Wigan ran out 13-9 winners.

Mick Sullivan goes around a Workington Town opponent at Wembley in 1958. Sullivan scored Wigan's first try in the seventeenth minute to level the scores, after the Cumbrians had taken an early lead.

Time Table and Programme of Music

1.30 pm to 2.20 pm
THE BAND OF THE PORTSMOUTH NAVAL COMMAND
(By permission of the Commander-in-Chief, Portsmouth)
THE BAND OF H.M. ROYAL MARINES
(Portsmouth Group)
(By permission of Major-General, Royal Marines, Portsmouth)
Director of Music : Captain K. A. McLean, M.B.E., L.R.A.M., R.M.

1. March	...	...	...	" Holyrood "	...	...	Alford
2. Selection	...	...	" The King and I "	...	...	Rodgers
3. Waltz	...	...	...	" España "	...	...	Waldteufel
4. March	...	...	" On the Quarter Deck "	...	...	Alford
5. Selection	...	...	" My Fair Lady "	...	...	Loewe
6. Selection	...	...	" Cavalcade "	...	...	Coward
7. Tango	...	...	...	" Blue Tango "	...	Leroy Anderson

2.20 pm to 2.50 pm
COMMUNITY SINGING
(Arranged by the Daily Express)
Conductor : ARTHUR CAIGER, D.C.M.
Accompanied by
THE BAND OF H.M. ROYAL MARINES
(Portsmouth Group)
THE NATIONAL ANTHEM

2.55 pm
PRESENTATION OF THE TEAMS TO
H.R.H. THE PRINCESS ROYAL

3.00 pm
Kick-off

3.40 pm
Half-time

MARCHING DISPLAY BY
THE MASSED BANDS OF H.M. ROYAL MARINES
COMPRISING
THE BAND OF THE PORTSMOUTH NAVAL COMMAND
(By permission of the Commander-in-Chief, Portsmouth)
THE BAND OF H.M.S. " ST. VINCENT "
(By permission of the Commander-in-Chief, Portsmouth)
THE BAND OF THE HOME FLEET
(By permission of the Commander-in-Chief, Home Fleet)
THE BAND OF H.M. ROYAL MARINES (Portsmouth Group)
(By permission of Major-General, Royal Marines, Portsmouth)
The Combined Bands under the direction of
Captain K. A. McLean, M.B.E., L.R.A.M., R.M., Director of Music, Portsmouth

4.30 pm
End of Match

Presentation of the Trophy and Medals
THE NATIONAL ANTHEM

(Cover photo by courtesy of Fox Photos Ltd.)

TODAY'S REFEREE—MR. CHARLES F. APPLETON (WARRINGTON)

Making his third appearance at Wembley. Refereed the Cup Finals of 1952 (Workington Town v. Featherstone Rovers) and 1957 (Leeds v. Barrow). Has over twenty international games and a visit to France for the 1954 R.L. World Cup games in his record. Hoped to become a professional soccer player but cartilage trouble cut short that aspiration.

Refereeing progress through the junior grades was rapid. Shortly after the war Mr. Appleton was appointed to the R.L. senior list. In his first senior season he was given charge of an England v. France game.

In business he is a commercial traveller with a Merseyside firm of chemical manufacturers.

5-1-13

★ ═══ **HULL** ═══ ★

(Colours: White Jerseys with Black V, Black Shorts)

Full back
A. KEEGAN (5 Goals)

2	3	4	5
Right wing three-quarter	*Right centre three-quarter*	*Left centre three-quarter*	*Left wing three-quarter*
S. COWAN	B. COOPER	B. SAVILLE	I. WATTS

6			7
Stand-off half-back			*Scrummage half-back*
G. MATTHEWS			T. FINN (Try)

8	9	10
Front row forward	*Hooker*	*Front row forward*
M. SCOTT	T. HARRIS	J. DRAKE

11		12
Second row forward		*Second row forward*
C. SYKES		W. D. DRAKE

Loose forward
13
J. WHITELEY
(C Capt.)

Referee:
Mr. C. F. APPLETON
(Warrington)

ATT: 79,811
REC: £33,098

Touch Judges:
H. SHAW (Oldham)
H. HUDSON (Dewsbury)

Loose forward
13
R. EVANS

12		11
Second row forward		*Second row forward*
N. CHERRINGTON		B. McTIGUE (Try)

10	9	8
Front row forward	*Hooker*	*Front row forward*
J. BARTON	W. SAYER	W. BRETHERTON

7			6
Scrummage half-back			*Stand-off half-back*
R. THOMAS			D. BOLTON (Try)

5	4	3	2
Left wing three-quarter	*Left centre three-quarter*	*Right centre three-quarter*	*Right wing three-quarter*
M. SULLIVAN (Try)	K. HOLDEN (Try)	E. ASHTON (Capt.)	Wm. J. BOSTON (2 Tries)

Full back
1
F. GRIFFITHS (6 Goals)

★ ═══ **WIGAN** ═══ ★

(Colours: Cherry and White Hooped Jerseys, White Shorts)

6-6-30

In the event of a draw after 80 minutes the Final Tie will be replayed at Odsal Stadium, Bradford, on Wednesday, May 13th, kick-off 7 pm. Seating tickets at 25/-, 15/-, 10/6 and 7/6, will be obtainable from the Rugby League Offices, Leeds; or Odsal Stadium ; or from Hull R.L.F.C. or Wigan R.L.F.C.

Scoring—A Try counts as 3 points. A Goal, however kicked, counts as 2 points. No goal can be kicked from a mark.

Wigan returned to Wembley in 1959 to face Hull, whose formidable pack had carried them to their first appearance in the stadium. The timetable indicated a truly 'royal' occasion as HRH The Princess Royal met the teams and presented the trophy.

Brian McTigue scores a Wigan try on the hour, effectively killing off a Hull comeback in the 1959 Challenge Cup final at Wembley. It crowned an outstanding display from McTigue, who took the Lance Todd award, as his side secured a spectacular 30-13 victory.

In 1958, the now-defunct *Rugby League Gazette* included a series of glossy photographs that featured the stars of the day, two of which are reproduced here. Tough-tackling wingman Mick Sullivan joined Wigan from Huddersfield for £9,500 in 1957. This move broke the Rugby League transfer record, exceeding the £5,000 Wigan had paid Dewsbury for Harry Street in 1951. Sullivan was a Wembley winner for Wigan in 1958 and 1959, and then had a third success – over Wigan – in 1961, after moving to St Helens for a new record fee of £11,000. A tourist in 1958 and 1962, his 48 appearances and 43 tries for Great Britain are both records. He also played 3 times for England and represented his native Yorkshire on 14 occasions.

MICK SULLIVAN
Gt. Britain and Wigan. Wing Three-quarter
R L Stars No 7   Issued by Rugby League Gazette, March 1958

BILLY BOSTON
Gt. Britain and Wigan. Wing Three-quarter
R. L. Stars. No. 1.   Issued by Rugby League Gazette, March 1958

Billy Boston, shown here in the Great Britain kit – for whom he played 32 times and scored 25 tries – toured Australia and New Zealand in 1954 and 1962. A Wales Rugby League side did not operate during his years in the game, although he did play twice for the Other Nationalities side against England and France in 1955 and scored 5 tries. Apart from his six Wembley appearances, he was in the Wigan team that won the 1960 Championship final over Wakefield Trinity. The block-busting winger's glittering career finished with 571 tries against his name, a figure only bettered in world Rugby League by Warrington's Brian Bevan. In October 1988, Boston became one of the original members of Rugby League's Hall of Fame.

South African scrum-half Tommy Gentles scores a spectacular try at Central Park, in a 38-0 demolition of Rochdale Hornets on 4 April 1959. Signed for £3,000 in 1958, the former Rugby Union international failed to establish himself and eventually went to Leeds for just £500 a year later.

Billy Boston kicks ahead at Leigh on 17 August 1960, in a match eventually won 25-9 by Wigan. The crowd of 21,500 for the visit of their derby rivals, was Leigh's biggest of the season. Wigan were defending their Championship title after beating Wakefield in the final just three months earlier, 27-3 at Odsal stadium, with Boston contributing two tries. The attendance of 83,190 was easily a record for a Championship decider.

One of the fastest pack men on Wigan's register during this period was second row forward Norman Cherrington, about to score one of his 80 tries for the club. He appeared in 257 games for Wigan between 1953 and 1962, including the 1958 and 1959 Wembley victories He made 2 international appearances, both of them in France. The first, for England, was in Lyons during May 1956, and was followed by selection for Great Britain in Toulouse in March 1960. He also represented Lancashire on 5 occasions between 1955 and 1957.

Rhodesian flyer Trevor Lake dives for the line to record his second try of the match for Wigan in a 14-14 home draw with Oldham on 3 November 1962.

THE RUGBY LEAGUE CHALLENGE CUP COMPETITION

FINAL TIE
ST. HELENS
v
WIGAN

SATURDAY, MAY 13th, 1961   KICK-OFF 3 p.m.

EMPIRE STADIUM

WEMBLEY

OFFICIAL PROGRAMME   ONE SHILLING

The third Wembley trip for Wigan in four seasons saw them up against their keenest rivals, St Helens, in a match where both sides were packed with star names.

Wigan left-winger Frank Carlton, who had been at Wembley with rivals St Helens five years previously, halts the progress of his opposite number, Tom van Vollenhoven, in the 1961 Challenge Cup final. A spectacular length-of-the-field effort, midway through the second half, ended with the Saints' South African speedster touching down, to confirm Wigan's 12-6 defeat.

Another Wembley-bound Wigan line-up, from 1963. From left to right, back row: John Barton, Frank Collier, Frank Carlton, Geoff Lyon, Brian McTigue, Billy Boston, Roy Evans, Jack Gregory. Front row: Alan Davies, David Bolton, Eric Ashton (captain), Frank Pitchford, Stan McCleod. This group shot was taken before the first round 7-0 victory at Hull on 7 March 1963. Gregory was deputizing at hooker for the unavailable Bill Sayer, but the latter played in the final.

Frank Carlton, in his third Wembley appearance in 1963, attempts to retrieve the ball after Wigan had kicked downfield, with Wakefield Trinity defenders Ian Brooke (left) and Colin Greenwood in contention. Trinity took the cup 25-10, after Wigan had failed to capitalize on first-half pressure.

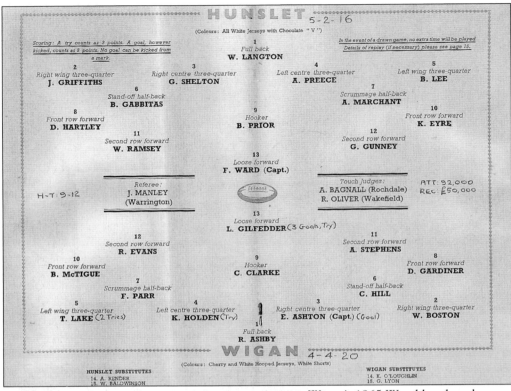

HUNSLET 5-2-16

(Colours: All White Jerseys with Chocolate " V ")

Scoring: A try counts as 3 points. A goal, however kicked, counts as 2 points. No goal can be kicked from a mark.

In the event of a drawn game, no extra time will be played
Details of replay (if necessary) please see page 15.

1
Full back
W. LANGTON

2 Right wing three-quarter **J. GRIFFITHS**

3 Right centre three-quarter **G. SHELTON**

4 Left centre three-quarter **A. PREECE**

5 Left wing three-quarter **B. LEE**

6 Stand-off half-back **B. GABBITAS**

7 Scrummage half-back **A. MARCHANT**

8 Front row forward **D. HARTLEY**

9 Hooker **B. PRIOR**

10 Front row forward **K. EYRE**

11 Second row forward **W. RAMSEY**

12 Second row forward **G. GUNNEY**

13 Loose forward **F. WARD (Capt.)**

H-T: 9-12

Referee:
J. MANLEY
(Warrington)

Touch Judges:
A. BAGNALL (Rochdale)
R. OLIVER (Wakefield)

ATT: 92,000
REC: £50,000

13 Loose forward **L. GILFEDDER** (3 Goals, Try)

12 Second row forward **R. EVANS**

11 Second row forward **A. STEPHENS**

10 Front row forward **B. McTIGUE**

9 Hooker **C. CLARKE**

8 Front row forward **D. GARDINER**

7 Scrummage half-back **F. PARR**

6 Stand-off half-back **C. HILL**

5 Left wing three-quarter **T. LAKE** (2 Tries)

4 Left centre three-quarter **K. HOLDEN** (Try)

3 Right centre three-quarter **E. ASHTON (Capt.)** (Goal)

2 Right wing three-quarter **W. BOSTON**

1
Full back
R. ASHBY

WIGAN 4-4-20

(Colours: Cherry and White Hooped Jerseys, White Shorts)

HUNSLET SUBSTITUTES
14. A. RENDER
15. W. BALDWINSON

WIGAN SUBSTITUTES
14. K. O'LOUGHLIN
15. G. LYON

Wigan's 1965 Wembley showdown with Hunslet produced what most experts considered to be the best final played at the famous venue up to that time.

Wigan loose-forward Laurie Gilfedder, shown here in his 1965 Wembley jersey, made a dramatic first appearance at the stadium. His penalty goal from the half-way line in the first minute remains the fastest ever scored at Wembley. The former Warrington star, who played 5 times for Great Britain, kicked 384 goals in 143 matches for Wigan.

Laurie Gilfedder looks for support, as he goes down in a tackle to Hunslet centre Alan Preece (4) watched by Hunslet loose-forward Fred Ward (right), at Wembley in 1965. Gilfedder's early second-half try for Wigan helped to keep a spirited Hunslet side at bay.

Trevor Lake scores a sensational try for Wigan on the hour in the 1965 final – adding to his first-half effort – by escaping the despairing tackle of Hunslet's John Griffiths. The move had started with a sizzling break by joint-Lance Todd Trophy winner Ray Ashby, who broke through a gap from his own 25-yard line, before transferring to Lake on the half-way line. It put Wigan in the driving seat at 20-9, but there were some tense moments, as Hunslet came back again before the Challenge Cup was secured with a 20-16 scoreline.

Trevor Lake patrolled Wigan's left flank for five seasons, following his arrival from Rhodesia in 1962. In 140 matches, he crossed for 132 tries, but the most memorable was his fabulous second-half effort at Wembley in 1965, which caught the imagination of Britain's sporting public, who saw the match live on BBC television.

Loose-forward Roy Evans (left, wearing Wigan's change strip) in action against Oldham at Central Park. Evans was a quick and strong player, who made his Wigan debut in 1957 and went on to appear 282 times for the club. He missed Wembley in 1958, due to illness, but made amends by appearing in four subsequent finals, two of which (1959 and 1965) ended in victory. He also shared in the 1960 Championship win. Evans toured in 1962 and represented Great Britain 4 times and Lancashire twice.

Wigan's sixth appearance at Wembley in nine years saw them re-matched with St Helens. The attendance of 98,536 created a record for a Rugby League Challenge Cup final at Wembley that has never been beaten.

THE RUGBY LEAGUE CHALLENGE CUP COMPETITION

FINAL
ST. HELENS
v
WIGAN

SATURDAY, MAY 21st 1966
Kick-off 3 p.m.

OFFICIAL PROGRAMME · · · · · ONE SHILLING

St Helens' John Mantle scores the opening try in the 1966 Challenge Cup final, despite the efforts of Trevor Lake (on ground). The other Wigan players are Eric Ashton (left) and Frank Parr. Wigan were badly handicapped by the suspension of hooker Colin Clarke. Utility player Tom Woosey deputized, but struggled against the experienced former Wigan number 9, Bill Sayer, as Saints ran out comfortable 21-2 winners.

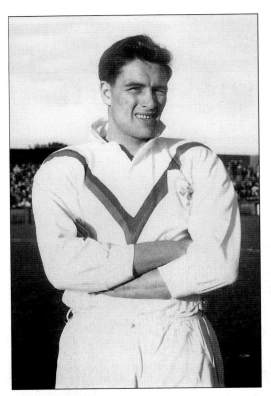

Eric Ashton is one of the classiest centres ever to represent Wigan, his partnership with Billy Boston being one of the most lethal combinations in Rugby League history. He signed for Wigan in 1955 and quickly established himself in the first team. His maturity and leadership qualities quickly led to the team captaincy, taking Wigan to six Wembley appearances and a memorable Championship win over Wakefield Trinity in 1960. In 1963, he was handed the extra responsibility of coach, and he continued to perform this role after retiring as a player in 1969, taking Wigan to Wembley again in 1970. His biggest honour was leading the Great Britain team to Australasia in 1962, having toured in 1958. He made 497 appearances for Wigan and represented Great Britain on 26 occasions, England once and Lancashire 10 times. In 1973, he left Central Park and later coached his hometown club, St Helens, whom he took to Wembley twice in the 1970s.

It is difficult to believe, when reflecting on the career of skilful ball-playing prop Brian McTigue, that he was signed by the club as a centre three-quarter – a position in which he made his first-team debut at the end of the 1950/51 campaign. After an uncertain start, he graduated to the pack as a back row forward, establishing himself at prop by 1956. Like Eric Ashton and Billy Boston, he was to add the 1960 Championship final success at Odsal to his six Wembley visits, playing in 422 matches for Wigan altogether. He toured in 1958 and 1962 and represented Great Britain 25 times and Lancashire 13. In 1967, he left Wigan, playing a match for Blackpool Borough in October before moving into a coaching role in Australia. His departure signalled not only the break-up of the Ashton/Boston/McTigue trio, but the fragmentation of what had been a truly exciting Wigan combination.

Five
The Sleeping Giant
1968-1980

With the Old Guard gone, coach Eric Ashton set about introducing new faces into the team, in an effort to keep Wigan at the forefront. By the early 1970s, it looked as if his mission was succeeding, as the team reached Wembley in 1970 and the Championship final in 1971. Fortunes declined, however, and Ashton left in 1973, to be succeeded by several coaches during an uncertain decade. It culminated in the unthinkable, when Wigan were relegated at the end of the 1979/80 season, the League having split into two divisions in 1973. Although beaten, the trip to Wembley in 1970, to meet Challenge Cup-holders Castleford, provided some respite. Here, we see Wigan centre Peter Rowe trying to avoid the clutches of Castleford's Bill Kirkbride, as colleague Bill Ashurst attempts to keep out of the way. Wigan skipper Doug Laughton looks on in the background.

Bill Francis was a product of Featherstone junior Rugby League, making his first appearance for Wigan in 1966. He played 400 times for the Cherry and Whites in a variety of back positions, primarily in the centre. He appeared in both the 1970 Challenge Cup final and the 1971 Championship final, experiencing the bitter pill of defeat both times. Solace came with wins in the Lancashire Cup (1971 and 1973) and the BBC2 Floodlit Cup (1968). Francis represented Great Britain on 4 occasions, Yorkshire 8 times and, through parental qualification, Wales 19 times. He moved to St Helens in October 1977, lining up for them later that season in the 1978 Challenge Cup final at Wembley, finishing with a runners-up medal again. Here, he leads out Brian Hogan and Denis Ashcroft at Central Park for the opening match of the 1975/76 season on 16 August against Widnes, who narrowly won 14-13.

Most pundits rate Bill Ashurst as Wigan's outstanding player of the 1970s. He began in 1968, playing mostly at centre, but made an impact when switched to the second row in 1969. His pace and power, allied to tactical kicking, was a revelation, and he formed an awesome back row with David Robinson and Doug Laughton. They provided the springboard that took Wigan to Wembley in 1970, and to the 1971 Championship decider with St Helens, which the Saints won narrowly, with Ashurst claiming the Harry Sunderland award as man of the match. He joined Australian side Penrith in 1973, returning to Wigan for the 1977/78 campaign. The reunion was brief, and he moved to Wakefield Trinity in March 1978 for a Rugby League record £18,000. With Trinity, he returned to Wembley in 1979, losing to Widnes. His representative career, curtailed by his decision to play in Australia, consisted of 3 Great Britain caps and 1 for Lancashire. He played 186 times for Wigan.

Cliff Hill made his Wigan debut in August 1964, after signing from the Newton-le-Willows Rugby Union Club. During his first three seasons at Central Park, he occupied the stand-off berth, the position he filled at Wembley in the Challenge Cup finals of 1965 and 1966. He was in the winning teams who claimed the Lancashire Cup in 1966 and the Floodlit Cup in 1968. After the arrival of his brother, David, he was employed more in the centre, returning to Wembley in 1970 as the first substitute used in the Challenge Cup final, coming off the bench to replace Colin Tyrer. He played 192 matches for the Cherry and Whites and represented Great Britain and Lancashire once each, both during the 1965/66 campaign.

David Hill joined his brother at Central Park in 1967, having previously played Rugby Union for Liverpool. He effectively took over at stand-off half, although, he too, was picked in the centre towards the end of his Wigan career. He made 329 appearances for the club, and was in the team that won the Lancashire Cup final against Widnes in 1971. He received runners-up medals in the 1970 Challenge Cup, 1971 Championship and 1969 BBC2 Floodlit Cup. Like his brother, he had a game each for Great Britain (1971) and Lancashire (substitute in 1969). He is seen here being tackled by a St Helens winger, Les Jones, in a Lancashire Cup clash at Knowsley Road on 7 September 1968, which Saints won 19-16.

THE RUGBY LEAGUE CHALLENGE CUP COMPETITION

FINAL

SATURDAY, MAY 9, 1970 Kick-off 3p.m.

CASTLEFORD V WIGAN

Official Programme   Two Shillings

EMPIRE **WEMBLEY** STADIUM

Eric Ashton's new-look Wigan side reached Wembley in 1970 to take on the cup-holders, Castleford. The Yorkshire side won a tight game 7-2 but, for Wigan, the most significant moment came in the sixteenth minute when Colin Tyrer was eliminated from the game after a late challenge. The loss of their prolific goalscorer was a major blow to the team.

Wigan's 1970 Wembley line-up. From left to right, back row: Colin Clarke, Keith Ashcroft, Bob Burdell, Bill Ashurst, John Stephens, Kevin O'Loughlin, Keri Jones, Cliff Hill. Front row: David Robinson, Frank Parr, Bill Francis, Doug Laughton (captain), Peter Rowe, Colin Tyrer, David Hill. The unlucky Stephens, who had played in all the cup rounds, sustained a hip injury and was replaced for the final by Brian Hogan. Hooker Clarke – a 1966 tourist – played in 436 matches for Wigan between 1963 and 1977, prop Stephens 238 (1963 to 1979) and scrum-half Parr 309 (1961 to 1972).

Wigan reached their first Championship final for eleven years in 1971, having led the League table by two points from St Helens and losing just four matches all season. It was the first time the two clubs had met in the Championship decider.

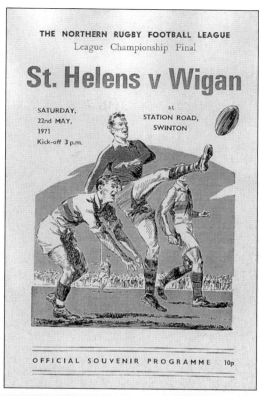

THE NORTHERN RUGBY FOOTBALL LEAGUE
League Championship Final

St. Helens v Wigan

SATURDAY,
22nd MAY,
1971
Kick-off 3 p.m.

at
STATION ROAD,
SWINTON

OFFICIAL SOUVENIR PROGRAMME   10p

David Robinson scores the only try of the first half for Wigan in the 1971 Championship final at Station Road, Swinton. An exciting match saw Wigan 12-6 ahead and looking favourites with seven minutes to go, but St Helens came back with two late tries to steal the win, 16-12.

The Wigan team before a match at Blackpool Borough on 26 August 1972, when they produced a 46-8 victory. From left to right, back row: Bill Ashurst, Denis Ashcroft, Colin Clarke, Bill Francis, Derek Watts, David Robinson. Front row: Kieron O'Loughlin, Chris Fuller, Warren Ayres, Doug Laughton (captain), David Hill, Billy Davies, Colin Tyrer. O'Loughlin was the younger brother of Kevin, who had played for the club at Wembley in 1970. Both gave outstanding service to the club during the 1970s, proving themselves reliable utility backs. Keiron appeared for Wigan 260 times – compared to Kevin's 309 – and later won a Challenge Cup winners medal for Widnes, against Wigan in 1984.

Colin Tyrer was an exciting, attacking full-back, joining Wigan from Leigh in 1967. He was a reliable goal-kicker and landed 813 in his 248 matches for the club, being renowned throughout the game for the meticulous care he took with his kicks, taking what seemed an eternity to opposing fans before starting his run-up. He won the Floodlit Cup with Wigan in 1968 and the Lancashire Cup in 1971 and was in the team beaten in the 1971 Championship final. His biggest disappointment was at Wembley in 1970 when a broken jaw – following a late challenge – meant an early exit. He played twice for the Great Britain under-24 side and 3 times for Lancashire. He transferred to Barrow in 1974.

Wigan win is the tipsters' pitfall

THE ART of tipping (horses, teams, etc., not monetary favours) is riddled with surprises, with traps and pitfalls.

In steeplechasing, no horse is a racing certainty to pass the winning post first unless there is only one nag in the field. And in competitive football either one of two teams can turn up trumps on the day.

Even so, there must have been a few shirts stuck on Salford for Saturday's Lancashire Cup Final.

Diehard Wiganers, the most optimistic of supporters, looked none too happy in the week before as their sorry-looking team fell slap happily at Leigh.

Yet, on the day, the form book was turned upside-down, inside out—and ripped into Red shreds as free-flowing Salford, the prolific points scorers in Rugby League, collapsed before the cherry - and - white wall of Wigan.

And this first final of the 1973/74 season looks like going down as the shock of the season.

Meanwhile, Wigan's glory grin is as wide as that of their great campaigner, Peter Smethurst, who picked up his first county winners medal in nigh on 20 years in the game.

And maybe the wise guys who wanted to sell the pies are now selling shirts!

As this newspaper report clearly indicates, Wigan caused an upset in defeating Salford in the 1973 Lancashire Cup final. Fortunes at Central Park were at a low ebb – the club just avoiding relegation – whilst Salford were in the midst of a Championship-winning campaign.

Peter Smethurst scores a try – only his second for Wigan – in a home match with Keighley on 19 April 1975. It should have been his farewell appearance, but he returned for one more outing in November 1977, when the club was short-handed. It was Smethurst, a Wembley winner with Leigh in 1971, who had inspired Wigan to their 19-9 Lancashire Cup victory in 1973 against his former club Salford. Although making just 49 appearances for Wigan at the end of a lengthy career, he later contributed to the Central Park cause by joining the coaching staff.

The Wigan team, before an unusual and subdued meeting with St Helens on 21 August 1976. The match, at Central Park, was a Lancashire Cup tie, but Saints fielded their reserve side, the first-team squad being on strike. The players are, from left to right, back row: Bernard Coyle, Tony Karalius, Brian Gregory, Bob Blackwood, Colin Clarke, Ray Martland (at back), Bob Irving, Denis Ashcroft. Front row: Kieron O'Loughlin, George Fairbairn, Jimmy Nulty, Alan Whittle, Bill Francis, Green Vigo, David Hill. Wigan won 37-5 in front of only 2,370 spectators. South African winger Vigo, signed from Saldhana Tigers Rugby Union Club in 1973, scored seven of Wigan's nine tries to equal the club record.

George Fairbairn proved an outstanding Rugby League full-back, after moving south of the border from Kelso Rugby Union Club in 1974. He played in 207 matches for Wigan – kicking 594 goals – taking over as player-coach in 1980, the year he won Rugby League's prestigious Man of Steel award. He was the only Wigan player involved in the 1979 tour Down Under, flying out as a replacement. He played 17 times for Great Britain and, although a Scot, represented England on 15 occasions and Lancashire twice. In 1981, he moved to Hull Kingston Rovers for a Rugby League record fee of £72,500, appearing for them at Wembley in 1986.

Six
The Maurice Lindsay Era
1981-2001

Wigan's Division One comeback in 1981, twelve months after being relegated, still left a mountain to climb, if the standard of past eras was to be repeated. Maurice Lindsay and Jack Robinson were two men who realized a revolution had to take place. That revolt began in November 1982 when a new four-man board – Lindsay, Robinson, Jack Hilton and Tom Rathbone (popularly referred to as 'The Gang of Four') – took control of club affairs. It is doubtful that even they, as ambitious as they were, dreamt of the unprecedented success to follow. Before the end of the twentieth century, an amazing forty-four trophy wins had accumulated – a spectacular run of eight consecutive Wembley victories and success in the World Club Challenge being the outstanding moments. The name of Wigan forced its way into the British sporting consciousness through sensational moments like Martin Offiah's spectacular Wembley try against Leeds in 1994, captured here as he out-manoeuvres former Widnes colleague Alan Tait.

Maurice Lindsay provided the leadership and vision that brought about Wigan's renaissance of the 1980s. Already an influential boardroom figure, he took over as chairman (from Jack Hilton) in 1988, continuing until 1992 when he left Central Park to take higher office as chief executive of the Rugby Football League and, from 1998, managing director – later chief executive – of Super League (Europe). In October 1999, he returned to his first love, resuming as Wigan chairman, Jack Robinson having been at the helm during most of Lindsay's absence. The reunion also coincided with the move from Central Park to the JJB Stadium, Dave Whelan becoming the major shareholder at the club in 1998. Lindsay, who was a key figure in the creation of Super League in 1995, was also president of the Rugby Football League in 1991/92. He was Great Britain tour manager in 1990 and 1992.

Alex Murphy leads the dressing-room celebrations after his team had won the John Player Trophy, defeating Leeds 15-4 in the final at Elland Road, Leeds, on 22 January 1983. It was Wigan's first silverware since lifting the Lancashire Cup in 1973. Murphy had taken over from Maurice Bamford as coach in June 1982 and made an early impact, taking his charges into third place in Division One during his first season in command and leading the team to Wembley in 1984 after a fourteen-year absence.

Henderson Gill was one of Wigan's earliest signings after gaining promotion, arriving in October 1981 from Rochdale Hornets for a reported £30,000 fee. The unorthodox style of wingman Gill provided the sparkle the 'new' Wigan needed – a crowd-pleaser that could draw the fans into Central Park. A member of the 1986/87 Championship team, he played his part in Wigan's first Premiership Trophy success that season. He appeared in three Challenge Cup finals (1984, 1985, 1988), scoring a sensational try in the 1985 win over Hull and received winning medals for the Lancashire Cup (1986, 1987) and John Player Trophy (1983, 1986, 1987). Gill was in the team for the memorable World Club Challenge win over Manly in 1987. He scored 145 tries and 106 goals in 226 appearances for Wigan. A tourist in 1988, he represented Great Britain (15 appearances), England (1) and Yorkshire (3). He transferred to Bradford Northern, his first senior club, in December 1989.

The signing of New Zealander Graeme West was a major coup for Wigan in November 1982. With 16 Test appearances under his belt, he had made an impression in the 1980 Kiwi tour of Britain, and as a member of their 1975 World Cup squad. At Wigan, the tall prop, or second row forward, proved an influential captain in an emerging team, appearing 202 times for the club. A member of the side that won the 1983 John Player final, he led the team that lost at Wembley in 1984, returning twelve months later to lift the cup. He was in the 1986/87 Championship-winning squad, handing the captaincy to Ellery Hanley mid-way through that campaign, and was skipper when the Lancashire Cup (1986) and John Player Trophy (1986 and 1987) were won. In May 1994, he took over as Wigan coach, a position he held for almost three years before a similar appointment at Widnes.

Colin Whitfield was captain of Wigan's victorious John Player Trophy side of 1983. A steadfast, intelligent centre, he arrived from Salford – in whose jersey he is seen here – in a player-exchange deal during November 1981, where he would reunite with former Salford coach, Alex Murphy. He was in the team that lost to Widnes at Wembley in 1984, missing the following season's triumphant return to the stadium, but back in the side for the Lancashire Cup final success over Warrington in 1985. Having appeared in 149 matches for Wigan, in which he registered 46 tries and 392 goals, he moved to Halifax in January 1986, with whom he returned to Wembley twice, sharing in their first Challenge Cup win since 1939 when St Helens were beaten in 1987. Whitfield made a single international appearance, for Great Britain under-24s against France at Villeneuve in January 1981, and represented Lancashire 5 times.

David Stephenson, a powerful, strong running centre, was a Wigan club record £60,000 signing from Salford in February 1982. It renewed his centre partnership with Whitfield and, similarly, would bring him once more under the influence of Alex Murphy. His greatest moment with Wigan was in winning the Challenge Cup at Wembley in 1985 and the World Club Challenge in 1987, when his four goals sealed a memorable 8-2 win over Manly-Warringah. Other triumphs with Wigan included the Premiership in 1987, the John Player Trophy (1983, 1986 and 1987) and the Lancashire Cup (1985, 1986 and 1987). In total, he played 214 times for Wigan, scoring 71 tries and 292 goals. He transferred to Leeds in January 1988, following which he was included in the 1988 tour party Down Under. He gained representative honours with Great Britain (10 times), Great Britain under-24s (5) and Lancashire (6).

Shaun Edwards, aged four, with father Jackie Edwards, the ex-Warrington half-back, at the 1971 Rugby League Challenge Cup final at Wembley. Edwards' early experience of the unique Wembley atmosphere must have made a strong impression on his young mind, although no one could have predicted his influence on the great day. As a player, he appeared in a record eleven finals with Wigan and London Broncos. After losing to Widnes in the 1984 final as the youngest ever Wembley finalist at seventeen years and six months, he returned a further nine times with Wigan and came away a winner every time! In 1988, he was the youngest Wembley captain at twenty-one years and six months. He concluded his love affair with the stadium in 1999, playing in the defeated Broncos side that went down to Leeds.

Apart from Wembley glory, Shaun Edwards, who signed in October 1983, enjoyed an exceptional Wigan career, winning eight Division One Championships (including seven in a row from 1989/90), five Premierships, seven John Player Trophy (renamed the Regal Trophy from 1990) finals, five Lancashire Cup finals, and three World Club Challenges. A supreme, tactical half, he was an influential player, his wonderful support play bringing him 274 tries in 467 appearances for Wigan. On 29 September 1992, he scored ten tries at Swinton, equalling Martin Offiah's club record of the previous May. In 1990, he took the Man of Steel award. He joined London Broncos in March 1997, transferring to Bradford Bulls seven months later, returning to the Broncos in July 1998. His skills were recognized through his 36 appearances for Great Britain, in whose livery he is shown here, and through his selection for two tours Down Under in 1988 and 1992.

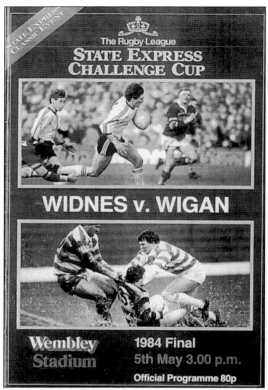

The Rugby League

STATE EXPRESS
CHALLENGE CUP

WIDNES v. WIGAN

Wembley Stadium

1984 Final
5th May 3.00 p.m.

Official Programme 80p

After a gap of fourteen years, Wigan fans were once more able to plan for a weekend in the capital as their emerging side took on Widnes, a team that had dominated the British game for almost ten years. Inspired by two Joe Lydon tries, the Chemics won 19-6 but, for many Wigan fans, it was just great to be involved in Rugby League's showpiece again.

Wigan made a quick return to Wembley, being involved in the 1985 classic against Hull. For many critics, it remains the greatest final ever staged, full of wonderful rugby and fabulous tries, Hull playing their part, despite losing 28-24. Apart from being a great advertisement for the sport, it was a clear signal that Wigan were back in the big time. Our picture shows Hull's Australian scrum-half Peter Sterling releasing the ball, under close scrutiny from Wigan's Ian Potter (left) and Brian Case.

The memory of Wembley in 1985 will always rekindle thoughts of two Australians who played with Wigan for that one season. John Ferguson was virtually unknown when signed on a short-term contract from Eastern Suburbs. Having set Central Park alight, he returned Down Under in February 1985, but agreement was reached for him to be flown halfway round the world to line up for Wigan in the cup final three months later. The exciting winger made his mark on the occasion with two sensational tries, the first of which sparked a comeback in the seventeenth minute, after Hull had led 6-0. His exploits with Wigan proved to be a platform to greater things on his return to Australia, where he won international recognition for his country and enjoyed Premiership glory with Canberra Raiders, meeting Widnes in the 1989 World Club Challenge. He played 25 matches for Wigan and scored 24 tries.

Brett Kenny was the first Australian player to win the Lance Todd Trophy, following his outstanding performance in the 1985 Challenge Cup final. His approach before the match appeared almost casual, but the classy stand-off gave one of the most inspired displays ever witnessed at Wembley. Here, he leaps high to beat the Hull defence in retrieving the ball during the final, with Mike Ford (7) in the foreground. An established international (he toured Britain in 1982 and 1986), Kenny was on the books of Parramatta, appearing in 25 matches for Wigan and scoring 19 tries.

Concentration on the Wigan bench, from left to right: Henderson Gill, Geoff Hurst (assistant coach), Graham Lowe (coach), Keith Mills (physiotherapist). New Zealander Lowe, who had coached his national side, took over from the Colin Clarke/Alan McInnes duo in August 1986. During his three seasons at the club, he revolutionized Wigan's style of play and, ultimately, that of the British game, presiding over two Wembley triumphs (1988 and 1989) and, perhaps his greatest achievement, capturing the World Club Challenge Trophy, after beating Manly in 1987.

Australian John Monie took over the coaching duties in September 1989, following Lowe's departure in June. Building on the foundations laid by his predecessor, his was to be the most successful spell of any coach in British Rugby League. He led the club to a Challenge Cup and Championship double in each of his four seasons, winning many other trophies along the way, including the 1991 World Club Challenge. He left in May 1993 to take an appointment with the newly formed Auckland Warriors. He returned to Wigan as coach in November 1997 (following spells in charge by John Dorahy, Graeme West and Eric Hughes) and, in 1998, took the team to Wembley once more, losing unexpectedly to Sheffield Eagles. He was offered a new role at Wigan, when his assistant Andy Goodway was invited by the board to step up as head coach in June 1999. Monie left, rejecting the idea, and later coached London Broncos.

Ellery Hanley, one of the sport's greatest ever players, arrived at Central Park in September 1985 from Bradford, for a Rugby League record £85,000. Switched from his usual centre-back position to loose-forward in February 1987, Hanley found new freedom to dictate and influence a game. As team captain, he led Wigan to the 1986/87 Championship and Premiership double and three consecutive victories at Wembley in 1989, 1990 and 1991, as well as being skipper for the historic win over Manly in 1987. He won the Man of Steel award three times (1985, 1987, 1989), the Lance Todd Trophy in 1989 and was awarded an MBE in 1990. His phenomenal try-scoring ability brought him 189 in 204 matches for Wigan, including 59 in 1986/87. He moved to Leeds in September 1991 for a new Rugby League record fee of £250,000, leading them to Wembley twice (1994, 1995). He toured three times (1984, 1988, 1992), as captain for the last two, and made 36 appearances for Britain. His coaching portfolio includes Britain, England and St Helens.

Wigan-born Andy Gregory grabbed a Wembley winners' medal in only his nineteenth start for Widnes in 1981, adding a second in 1984 against Wigan. He transferred to Warrington in January 1985 in a player-exchange deal, joining Wigan two years later for £130,000. A pocket battleship of a scrum-half, he was an inspirational player who could control the pattern of a game. One of his finest moments with Wigan was captaining the team that won the World Club Challenge against Penrith in 1991, having been in the team that beat Manly in 1987. He added to his Wembley haul with five consecutive wins from 1988, claiming the Lance Todd Trophy in 1988 and 1990. He went on three tours (1984, 1988, 1992) and was selected 25 times for Britain plus 8 for Lancashire. In August 1992, having played 182 times in a Wigan jersey, he went to Leeds for £30,000, ending his career as player-coach of Salford.

Merlin trading cards were a welcome addition for collectors during 1991/92. The 160-card set included 12 featuring Wigan, 4 of which are reproduced on this and the facing page. Dependable full-back Steve Hampson was signed in October 1983 from the Vulcan Rugby Union Club. After a particularly unlucky period that saw him miss three Wembley finals through injury, he shared the glory of victory at the stadium for five successive years from 1989. He also secured winning medals for the Premiership Trophy twice, the John Player/Regal Trophy four times, the Lancashire Cup five times, and the World Club Challenge in 1987 and 1991. A tourist in 1992, he appeared 12 times for Great Britain and 3 for Lancashire. He took part in 304 matches with Wigan before, in July 1993, he transferred to Halifax.

Martin Dermott was a local signing from Wigan St Patrick's in November 1984. The skilful, ball-playing hooker was the only other player (besides Shaun Edwards) to feature in Wigan's eight Division One Championship squads between 1986/87 and 1995/96. He also shared in the club's success in the Challenge Cup (five times), John Player/Regal Trophy (five), Lancashire Cup (three) and the Premiership Trophy win of 1992. He played in three of Wigan's World Club Challenge clashes, winning in 1991 and 1994. In total, he appeared in 231 games for the Central Park club. His talent was recognized with 11 appearances for Great Britain and 2 for Lancashire and he was included in the tour parties of 1990 and 1992. He joined Warrington in January 1997.

New Zealand centre Dean Bell played for Carlisle in 1982/83 and Leeds in 1983/84, returning Down Under to join Eastern Suburbs. Wigan tempted him back in September 1986, his reputation as an uncompromising three-quarter earning the title 'Mean Dean'. He was a Wembley winner seven times and captain in 1992, 1993 (taking the Lance Todd Trophy at loose-forward) and 1994. He gained winners' medals for the Division One Championship, the Premiership, John Player/Regal Trophy and Lancashire Cup. His biggest disappointment was leading the side that lost the 1992 World Challenge to Brisbane Broncos. Personal accolades include captaining New Zealand, the Man of Steel award in 1992 and being the subject of television's *This is Your Life* in 1993. He appeared for Wigan in 253 matches, scoring 105 tries. After the 1993/94 season, he joined John Monie at Auckland Warriors, returning to coach Leeds from September 1995 for two years before joining the back-room staff at Wigan in November 1999.

DEAN BELL

WIGAN

ANDY GOODWAY

WIGAN

Andy Goodway was a tough-tackling back row forward who arrived from Oldham for £60,000 in July 1985. Already an established Great Britain international, having been on the 1984 tour, he was to represent Britain 23 times. Within months of signing for Wigan he had the honour of captaining his new colleagues in the 34-8 Lancashire Cup final win over Warrington, the first of four successes he enjoyed with Wigan in that competition. In 1987, he was a winner in two 'firsts' with Wigan – the inaugural World Club Challenge and the first Premiership final staged at Old Trafford. He was also in the winning side in the Challenge Cup and John Player/Regal Trophy on four occasions apiece. He played 224 times for Wigan, transferring to Leeds in August 1992 before moving into coaching, a role that saw him in charge of Great Britain and, eventually, Wigan, holding the reins from June to November 1999.

Joe Lydon, a three-quarter with exceptional pace who could play full-back or stand-off, was another Wigan lad who founded his career at Widnes. He proved a handful for Wigan at Wembley in 1984, his two spectacular tries taking the cup to Widnes, earning him the Lance Todd Trophy and rubber-stamping his 1984 Man of Steel accolade. Returning 'home' to Wigan for a Rugby League record £100,000 in January 1986, he won Championship honours in his first full season (1986/87), crowning that by taking the Harry Sunderland Trophy in Wigan's Premiership victory over Warrington. He was in two World Club Challenge winning teams (1987, 1991), and added five Wembley winners medals. His Wigan career covered 262 matches, 90 tries, and 309 goals. Lydon toured in 1984, 1990 and 1992, making
31 appearances for Britain. After retiring, he joined the Wigan coaching staff, before accepting the position of Technical Director for the RFL, later taking up a coaching role with the England RFU.

Andy Platt was another big-name signing, arriving from St Helens for £140,000 in September 1988. Originally a second row forward (a position he occupied during Saints' 1987 Wembley appearance), Platt developed into one of the toughest props in the game. In 1992, he won the Harry Sunderland Trophy as top performer in the Premiership final against his old club and, a year later, was honoured with the Man of Steel award. He gained winners' medals in six consecutive Challenge Cup finals (1989 to 1994), the Lancashire Cup (1988, 1992) and Regal Trophy (1990, 1993). He appeared 200 times for Wigan (his final season being 1993/94), before joining the Central Park exodus to Auckland Warriors. In 1995, he returned home and played for Widnes, joining Salford in 1996 then, two years later, becoming Workington Town's player-coach. He received 25 caps for Great Britain and was a tourist in 1988 and 1992.

Wigan claimed their first Rugby League Championship for twenty-seven years by taking the Division One crown in 1986/87. It was a feat they would emulate from 1989/90 until 1995/96, thereby becoming Champions for seven consecutive seasons – a record for the British game. Here, the team celebrate with their much-prized trophy and an oversized cheque from competition sponsors, Stones Bitter. From left to right, back row: Dean Bell, Ray Mordt, Brian Case, Shaun Wane, Ian Potter, Graeme West, David Stephenson, Graham Lowe (coach), Nicky Kiss. Front row: Henderson Gill, Shaun Edwards, Andy Gregory, Ellery Hanley, Andy Goodway, Joe Lydon, Steve Hampson.

The Rugby Football League came up with a masterstroke when they transferred the Premiership Trophy event to Old Trafford, setting up a 'double header' with the newly created Second Division Premiership. It immediately raised the status of the end-of-season finale and the crowd at the final was treble the size of the previous year's attendance, creating the forerunner of the modern Super League Grand Final. In wet conditions, Wigan won their first Premiership title 8-0, recapturing the crown five times during the 1990s.

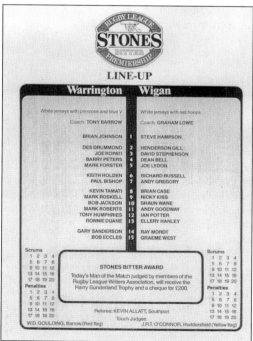

Back at Wembley in 1988 for the third time in five finals, and looking capable of emulating the cup exploits of the great side of the late 1950s/early 1960s, nobody foresaw that Wigan was at the dawn of an unbelievable eight consecutive victories at the famous Twin Towers. Here, the players joyously show off their trophy, after defeating holders Halifax 32-12. From left to right, back row: Geoff Hurst (assistant coach), Ian Potter, Andy Goodway, Ellery Hanley, Shaun Wane, Kevin Iro, Joe Lydon, Henderson Gill. Front row: Brian Case, Tony Iro, Nicky Kiss, Shaun Edwards, Steve Hampson (unable to play due to injury), Dean Bell (obscured by Ged Byrne's arm who, in turn, is hidden behind Hampson), Andy Gregory. Prop Adrian Shelford was just out of shot.

Ellery Hanley scores against St Helens at Wembley in 1989 during the twenty-sixth minute. It followed a sensational run by the Wigan skipper, who had evaded five would-be tacklers before touching down behind the posts, after accepting a pass just inside the Saints' half. It was the third time that the two famous rivals had clashed at the stadium, Wigan reversing the two previous results with an emphatic 27-0 scoreline.

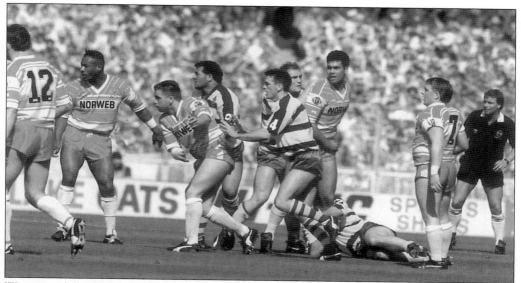

Wigan made history in 1990 as the first side to win three consecutive Challenge Cup finals, as they overcame Warrington 36-14. Wigan hooker Martin Dermott (centre of the picture), making his Wembley debut, gets the ball away despite the attentions of Paul Derbyshire (4). Other Wigan players are, from left to right: Andy Goodway (12), Ellery Hanley, Kevin Iro and Andy Gregory (7). For the third year in a row, Iro came tantalizingly close to becoming the first player to notch a 'hat-trick' of tries at Wembley, scoring two on each occasion.

Wigan met St Helens at Wembley for the fourth time in 1991 and entered the record books as the first club to reach four consecutive Challenge Cup finals. Wigan narrowly won 13-8 in the least convincing of their Wembley performances in this period – possibly a reflection of an end-of-season schedule that had them playing ten matches in just over a month, players carrying injuries into the match as a result. Captain Ellery Hanley famously had a late fitness check on the pitch, under the gaze of the television cameras, an hour before kick-off! Thankfully, his hamstring received the 'all-clear'. Our picture shows Wigan's Martin Dermott looking for support whilst being tackled by a Saints defender, with colleague and prop Ian Lucas preparing to lend a hand.

It was 'party time' yet again in 1992 for Wigan players and officials, after beating Castleford 28-12 at Wembley. For captain Dean Bell (behind the trophy) it was a special moment, as he had just captained the team to victory for the first time, having taken over from the departed Ellery Hanley. Bell was destined to lead Wigan to Wembley glory three years running, thus emulating Hanley's achievement.

Wembley 1993 and, this time, Widnes – the cup kings of the 1970s and '80s – provided the opposition. Andy Farrell, who had entered the fray as a fifty-fifth minute substitute for Kelvin Skerrett, hands off Widnes wingman John Devereux. Still only seventeen years and eleven months old, Farrell became the youngest player to receive a winners' medal at Wembley, Wigan finishing on top 20-14.

A feeling of disbelief overcomes Martin Offiah, as he sinks to his knees after scoring what is probably the most memorable try ever seen at Wembley. It came in the fourteenth minute of the 1994 Challenge Cup final against Leeds. Taking a pass from under his own posts, he had burst through the Leeds defensive line to race the length of the pitch, outwitting Leeds full-back Alan Tait to go in at the corner. It was an incredible solo effort, setting Wigan on the road to a 26-16 victory, Offiah receiving the Lance Todd Trophy for the second time.

For the second year running, Leeds provided the opposition in 1995 for what would be the finale of Wigan's incredible run of Wembley wins. Second row forward Denis Betts, making his seventh appearance in the final (having been a Lance Todd Trophy recipient in 1991), bursts through the Leeds defence. Wigan signed off in style, as the Yorkshire side was overwhelmed 30-10.

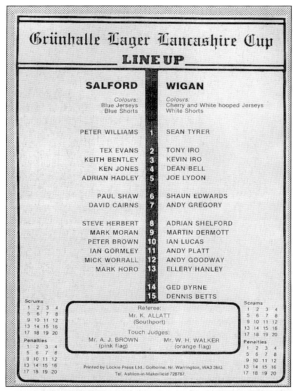

Wigan was starting to dominate the Lancashire Cup, winning for the fourth successive year in 1988 after defeating Salford 22-17 at St Helens. The turning point occurred during a blistering five-minute spell late in the game, when Wigan registered three tries. It was the club's best run in the competition since the early post-war years, when they had kept the trophy for six seasons.

Wigan celebrate winning the Lancashire Cup in 1992, after defeating St Helens 5-4, with all of their points coming from the boot of Frano Botica (two penalties and a drop goal). It was to be the last time that this historic trophy was competed for, Wigan having won the first contest in 1905. The Cherry and Whites certainly left their mark, having appeared in 35 finals, winning 21 of them – both figures being competition records by some distance.

Outstanding second row Denis Betts signed from Leigh Rangers in October 1986. Over the years, he made a big impact in the hunt for silverware, his medal collection including the Championship (six times), Challenge Cup (seven), Premiership Trophy (three), John Player/Regal Trophy (four) and Lancashire Cup (two). He featured in three World Club Challenge matches, winning two of them. He joined Auckland Warriors in 1995 on a reported five-year contract, but returned to Wigan in 1998, finding himself back at Wembley the same year, losing to Sheffield. He suffered further reversals as a member of the 2000 and 2001 Super League Grand Final side. On a personal level, he received the Lance Todd Trophy (1991) and Man of Steel (1995). He made 32 appearances in the Great Britain jersey, including three tours (1990, 1992 and 1996), the latter when he was on the books of Auckland. At the end of 2001, his two spells at Wigan had covered 367 matches.

The evening of Wednesday 7 October 1987, witnessed one of the most memorable matches in the history of Wigan and British Rugby League in general – still coming to terms with the near-invincibility of the 1982 and 1986 Kangaroos. The inaugural World Club Challenge staged at Central Park pitted British Champions, Wigan, against Australian Premiers, Manly-Warringah, with Wigan coach Graham Lowe adding to the sense of occasion by selecting an all-English line-up (the exception being New Zealand substitute Graeme West, who was not used). A massive 36,895 crowd witnessed an emotionally charged encounter, as Wigan won 8-2 on the back of four David Stephenson penalty goals. Here, we see Shaun Edwards on the break urged on by captain Ellery Hanley (left), as Manly's Cliff Lyons attempts to cover.

Wigan's second tilt at the World Club Challenge was in October 1991, when they met Penrith Panthers at Liverpool Football Club's Anfield ground. Despite a determined effort by the Australian champions, Wigan won comfortably at 21-4. Denis Betts, having changed into a Penrith jersey, shows off the trophy to ecstatic fans.

Coach John Monie, surrounded by his happy squad of players and backroom staff, takes hold of the Foster's World Club Challenge Trophy after the 1991 victory. His team was clearly eager to snap up a Penrith jersey each as a souvenir of the occasion, with all seventeen players sporting the Aussie club's black and white strip.

In June 1994, Wigan regained their world crown in impressive style at the ANZ Stadium in Brisbane, beating the Brisbane Broncos 20-14 in a dramatic encounter. Watched by a 54,220 crowd, it was a case of sweet revenge for Wigan, having relinquished the title to the Broncos in 1992, following a 22-8 defeat at Central Park. The *Daily Telegraph* correspondent, John Whalley, described the performance as 'one of the most outstanding achievements in the history of the British game'.

By John Whalley
in Brisbane

BRITISH CHAMPIONS ON TOP OF WORLD WITH RUGBY LEAGUE VICTORY DOWN UNDER

Wigan unite to buck the Broncos

Kings in Queensland ... the victorious Wigan team begin their celebrations in Brisbane   Picture: JOE MANN

Brisbane .... 14 pts
Wigan........................20

WITH a defensive display which can rarely have been equalled by a British side, Wigan took the World Club Challenge with a narrow but thoroughly deserved victory over the Australian champions yesterday.

At times Wigan showed the wear and tear of a gruelling 45-game British season. There was also a 25-minute period in the second half, when the Brisbane pressure was at its most intense, that it seemed certain Wigan's heroic rearguard would disintegrate.

But, overall, Wigan did what they set out to do. They took the three try-scoring chances which came their way, kept their heads in a game high in handling errors and, for the most part, stopped Brisbane offloading the ball in advanced attacking positions.

They also showed they could match Australia's best in terms of fitness with the excellent back three of Phil Clarke, Denis Betts and Andrew Farrell more than equal to their Brisbane counterparts, while Shaun Edwards, Jason Robinson and Gary Connolly were the pick of the backs.

Wigan have taken the world champions title twice before, in 1987 and 1991, but both those successes were achieved in England. Winning on Australian soil before a partisan crowd of more than 54,000 must rank as one of the outstanding achievements in the history of the British game.

In the past, the Australians have pointed out that

the Challenge has been played at the end of their domestic season but there can be no doubting the merit or significance of this result.

As Betts was quick to point out: "We've heard nothing else but how superior the Australians are and how we have only beaten them in the past because of the venue and the timing of the challenge.

"They can't say that anymore. They've had their chance on their own patch midway through their season and at the end of ours. We have won three competitions this season and each supplies it own satisfaction but this victory is something we've worked tremendously hard for."

It was vital Wigan scored first and, thanks to an error by Willie Carne, who was badly positioned to field Edwards' bomb, Betts supplied it by reacting first as the ball bounced over the line in the seventh minute.

Nine minutes later, Clarke sent Barrie-Jon Mather away and the centre easily beat Steve Renouf and used Martin Offiah as a decoy to drift past Wendell Sailor for the second try.

Robinson, Sam Panapa, Offiah and Connolly all made try saving tackles before Sailor replied for Brisbane in the 27th minute going outside Offiah to score in the corner.

But, while Frano Botica added both goals for Wig-

an's tries, Julian O'Neill was unsuccessful with the conversion and when Michael Hancock spilled the ball for Robinson to collect and cross in the 34th minute, Wigan looked set to take the title in comfort.

But, it only signalled a fierce attacking onslaught from Brisbane which, even two years ago, would surely have seen an English club defence wilt.

However, though they pulled tries back through Hancock (46 mins) and O'Neill 13 minutes later, with the latter adding one goal, Wigan regained their composure and Botica stretched the lead to six points after a Carne foul on Betts 14 minutes from time.

Brisbane: Sailor, Hancock, Renouf (Ryan 23), Johns, Carne; Kevin Walters (Plath 8, McKenna 74), Langer, Lazarus, Kennel, Walter, Gee (Gates 65), Hohn, Cann, O'Neill.

Wigan: Connolly, Robinson, Panapa, Mather (Atcheson 81), Offiah, Botica, Edwards, Cowie, Dermott (Hall 24), McGinty (Cassidy 27), Betts, Farrell, Clarke.

Referee: G McCallum (Sydney).

● Auckland are expected to announce the signing of Botica tomorrow. Betts is also expected to confirm he will be joining the club, but both will stay at Wigan until the end of next season.

● Widnes have transferlisted Great Britain forward Paul Moriarty, who is wanted by Workington, and New Zealand Test player Esene Faimalo, who looks likely to join Leeds. Both have been valued at £190,000 after turning down new contract offers.

Andy Farrell places the ball, before kicking one of his 1,037 goals from 288 appearances for Wigan. Signed from Orrell St James in October 1992, he became Britain's youngest Test forward at eighteen years five months, opposing New Zealand in November 1993. In 1996, he captained Britain's tour Down Under, won the Man of Steel and took the Harry Sunderland Trophy in the Premiership final win over St Helens. He repeated the Sunderland award in the 1997 Premiership, Saints again being runners-up. The youngest Wembley winner in 1993, further honours at the Twin Towers came in 1994 and 1995. His return in 1998, as skipper, was less fruitful, as Sheffield pulled off a surprise win. A member of the team that won the World Club Challenge in 1994, he has four Premiership winners' medals, and led Wigan in three Super League Grand Finals (1998, 2000 and 2001), winning the former. His 429 points in 2001 broke Frano Botica's eight-year-old club record. Prior to the Autumn 2001 Test series against Australia, he had 19 caps for Britain.

Martin Offiah made a sensational start with Widnes, whom he joined from Rosslyn Park RU in 1987, taking the Man of Steel award in 1988 and setting a Widnes high of 58 tries in 1988/89. A Rugby League record £440,000 brought the dazzling winger to Central Park in January 1992. Four months later, he scored a club record ten tries in the Premiership semi-final against Leeds on 10 May 1992, his Wigan count reaching an impressive 186 in 159 appearances. He was in Wigan's side that took the World Club title in 1994, having won with Widnes in 1989, and claimed four Challenge Cup winners' medals in Wigan colours, taking the Lance Todd accolade in 1992 and 1994. He transferred to London Broncos in August 1996, losing at Wembley with them in 1999, and then joined Salford in 2000. He toured in 1988, 1990 and 1992, and made 33 appearances for Great Britain.

Neil Cowie, signed from Rochdale Hornets in September 1991, developed into one of the most consistent and workmanlike props ever for Wigan, playing in 330 matches for the club. His list of successes at Wigan include the Division One Championship (five times), Challenge Cup (two), Premiership Trophy (five), Regal Trophy (three), Lancashire Cup (one), World Club Challenge (two) and the Super League Grand Final (one). He toured in 1992, and has represented Great Britain 3 times and played for Wales on 6 occasions.

1992 Lions Tour

Wigan had a Rugby League club record thirteen players on the 1992 tour, beating the previous best (also by Wigan) of eight in 1950. The players are, from left to right, back row: Steve Hampson, Neil Cowie, Denis Betts, Martin Offiah, Kelvin Skerrett, Shaun Edwards. Front row: Phil Clarke, Joe Lydon, Andy Gregory, Billy McGinty, Andy Platt, Martin Dermott, Ian Lucas. A fourteenth player, winger David Myers, was flown out in mid-tour as a replacement. Ten of them appeared together in the First Test against Australia, whilst in the Second (a memorable 33-10 win in Melbourne) and Third Tests, the entire pack was composed of Wigan players.

Frano Botica made 7 appearances with the All Blacks, before switching codes to join Wigan in June 1990. A half-back in Rugby Union, he was used mostly by Wigan as a wing three-quarter, but it was his uncannily accurate goal-kicking that will be remembered. It seemed not to matter where he took his kicks from, the result was always the same, setting Wigan records of 186 goals (1994/95) and 423 points (1992/93). His total for Wigan covered 840 in 179 matches, landing ten in the Premiership finals of 1992 and 1995. He was a Challenge Cup winner five times, and was in the 1991 and 1994 teams that won the World Club Challenge. In 1995, along with colleagues Dean Bell, Denis Betts and Andy Platt, he joined John Monie at Auckland Warriors. Back in England in 1996, he signed for Castleford, before returning to Rugby Union with Orrell.

Va'aiga Tuigamala signed from New Zealand's Ponsonby Rugby Union Club in January 1994, a considerable coup for Wigan at the time, such was the reputation of the player who had made 19 appearances for the All Blacks. A big, strong, rampaging three-quarter, he soon earned the name of 'Inga the Winger', although he eventually moved to centre where he could do more damage. Tuigamala played his part in winning the Challenge Cup at Wembley in 1994 and 1995, the Regal Trophy (1995 and 1996) and the Premiership Trophy (1996). His stay was relatively short (102 appearances and 62 tries), moving to Newcastle Rugby Union Club for a reported £750,000 in February 1997. A vastly improved player after joining Wigan, he caught the eye of the RFU in Wigan's free-flowing Middlesex Sevens side at Twickenham in 1996, followed by a period with Wasps during the 1996/97 winter break.

Jason Robinson signed from the Hunslet-Parkside club in July 1991 as a promising half-back, but with first-team chances limited, coach John Monie brought him into the side on the wing. His explosive, evasive, running style, that earned him the name 'Billy Whizz', proved a match-winning quality for club and country (he represented Great Britain 12 times). He was in Wigan's Wembley winning sides of 1993 and 1995, taking the Lance Todd Trophy in 1995, adding the Harry Sunderland award, after his try steered the first Super League Grand Final Wigan's way in 1998. He also received winners' medals for the Premiership, Regal Trophy and Lancashire Cup, and was in the team that won the 1994 World Club Challenge. Having scored 171 tries in 281 matches, he made national sporting headlines by joining Sale Rugby Union Club in October 2000, leading to his inclusion in the British Lions RU tour to Australia in 2001.

Gary Connolly emerged as an outstanding talent after he broke into St Helens' side at full-back in the late 1980s. He appeared in both the Saints sides that lost to Wigan at Wembley in 1989 and 1991, and was a tourist in 1992, before transferring to Central Park in July 1993 for £250,000, as a readymade replacement for Steve Hampson. It was in the centre, however, that Wigan found his strength and speed most effective. He gained his elusive Challenge Cup winners' medal as a member of Wigan's successful 1994 and 1995 teams, achieving further headlines in winning the 1994 World Club Challenge. He enhanced his medal set with wins in the Premiership Trophy, Regal Trophy and the inaugural Super League Grand Final of 1998. Prior to the 2001 Tests with Australia, his international honours include 23 caps for Great Britain. He has played 268 times for Wigan, contributing 129 tries.

Henry Paul came to Britain in October 1993 as captain of the Junior Kiwis, and was drafted into the senior New Zealand side (touring at the same time) for 4 matches. Wakefield Trinity saw his potential and he signed for them in December 1993, playing 19 matches that season, including an outstanding display at Wigan, alerting the club to his talents. He returned home to Auckland Warriors, but a deal was reached and he signed with Wigan in July 1994. Playing initially at full-back, he received winning medals in 1995 for the Challenge Cup, Premiership Trophy and Regal Trophy. Moving to his more accustomed stand-off position, he continued to win honours, including the 1998 Super League Grand Final. With 147 appearances for Wigan under his belt, he joined Bradford Bulls for 1999, representing them in the Challenge Cup finals of 2000 and 2001 but, midway through the 2001 campaign, his defection to Gloucester Rugby Union Club was announced.

The month of May 1996 was an historic one for rugby in England, as this poster testifies. Wigan's Va'aiga Tuigamala (left) happily accepts a blow from Bath captain Phil de Glanville in the build-up to a contest that would have been impossible months earlier. A century of division disappeared overnight, following the RFU's decision to adopt professional status, and the first of two cross-code challenge matches between the clubs took place at Manchester City's Maine Road stadium. Played on 8 May under Rugby League rules, Wigan won comfortably 82-6.

The second meeting between Wigan and Bath – under Rugby Union rules – took place at Twickenham on 25 May. Watched by a 42,000 crowd, the two teams march out onto the hallowed turf led by captains Andy Farrell (left) and Bath's Phil de Glanville. Bath won 44-19, after Wigan made the score respectable with three late tries. In between the two meetings, Wigan had taken part in the Middlesex Sevens – also at Twickenham – on 11 May. The Cherry and Whites went all the way and defeated Wasps 38-15 in the final in front of an attendance of 61,000.

The Merlin sticker collection was issued for the 1997 Super League campaign, the club's first season as Wigan Warriors. The set contained 325 stickers, 25 devoted to Wigan, a couple of which are reproduced on this page. Mick Cassidy, an excellent clubman, had his loyalty recognized with a testimonial beginning in May 2000, ten years after signing from Wigan St Judes. At the conclusion of the 2001 term, he had played in 292 matches for the club. The industrious back row forward has appeared in Challenge Cup and Regal Trophy-winning teams twice each and the Premiership four times. He was in the line-ups that won the 1994 World Club Challenge in Brisbane and the 1998 Super League Grand Final at Old Trafford. His international career includes appearances for Great Britain, England, and Ireland whilst, in 1996, he was in the British squad that toured the Southern Hemisphere.

Kris Radlinski has proved an exceptional local find, equally effective at full-back or centre. A product of the club's outstanding Academy team, he signed professionally in May 1993 at seventeen. He crowned his first full season in the first team by taking the Harry Sunderland Trophy in the 1995 Premiership final, scoring a hat-trick of tries as Wigan massacred Leeds 69-12. He enjoyed further Premiership wins in 1996 and 1997, and in the Regal Trophy for 1996. He has played in three Super League Grand Finals, winning in 1998. His one Challenge Cup final experience was the 1998 loss to Sheffield. His career record includes 219 appearances for Wigan (scoring 130 tries), 14 for Great Britain – prior to the 2001 Tests against Australia – and 9 for England. He was also in the Great Britain squad to New Zealand and the South Pacific in 1996.

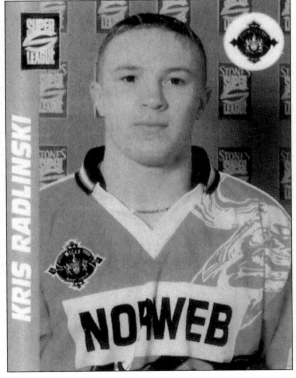

Action from the first ever *Super League* Grand Final in 1998, as Wigan second row Lee Gilmour looks for an opening in the Leeds defence, supported by captain and loose-forward Andy Farrell (right). Wigan came back to win 10-4 after an early Leeds try. The top five play-off concept caught the imagination of the fans, with the 43,553 attendance for the final at Old Trafford exceeding all previous turnouts for the decider in the deposed Premiership competition.

Wigan reached their second *Super League* Grand Final in 2000 at Old Trafford, but had to be content with finishing second-best to St Helens, who won 29-16. Kris Radlinski, who played centre, takes on the Saints loose-forward, Paul Sculthorpe, with Wigan skipper Andy Farrell (right) keeping an eye on things. Twelve months later, the Warriors again fell at the final hurdle, losing 37-6 to Bradford Bulls in front of a record 60,164 crowd.

The final match staged at Central Park on 5 September 1999. Andy Farrell makes a powerful break against traditional rivals St Helens, watched by a sell-out all-ticket crowd of 18,179. Wigan won 28-20 on a day of many emotions. Two weeks later, the Cherry and Whites made their debut at their new home, the JJB Stadium, but unexpectedly lost in the opening match of the Super League play-offs to Castleford, 14-10. It was the first time since the 1983/84 season that there were no new exhibits for the trophy cabinet.

A panoramic action picture illustrating the spectacular setting of the magnificent new JJB Stadium. Completed in August 1999, and shared with Wigan Athletic Football Club, the stadium took its name from the company owned by Dave Whelan, who became the major shareholder – and saviour – of Wigan Rugby League Club in 1998. Wigan's Australian centre, Steve Renouf, scores against Warrington under the glare of the floodlights in the opening match of the 2001 Super League season. Played on 2 March, Wigan got their campaign off to a positive start with a 34-6 victory in front of 11,138 fans.